Metatheatre

A New View of Dramatic Form

by

LIONEL ABEL

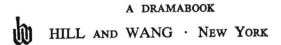

A DRAMABOOK

HILL AND WANG · NEW YORK

FIRST EDITION JANUARY 1963

Manufactured in the United States of America by
The Colonial Press, Clinton, Massachusetts

To Sherry Abel

Preface

I HAVE TRIED in this book to do two things: one, to explain why tragedy is so difficult, if not altogether impossible, for the modern dramatist, and two, to suggest the nature of a comparably philosophic form of drama. In other words, I have tried to shut one door more or less firmly and to open another door just a little. Beyond the door I have tried to open are a number of masterpieces dating back to the sixteenth century; there are also great contemporary works. And I believe the plays which will occupy us in the future will in their general structure and philosophy be like these.

I have also given a name to the kind of plays which have been, and will be, I think, important to us. Perhaps a better name than the one I elected for can be suggested. I do not insist that the name I have proposed ought to be adopted. But I do insist that the kind of plays I have designated as metatheatre needs designation.

After Aristotle, Hegel, and Nietzsche, it should be possible to talk with some degree of clarity about tragedy. Yet that dramatic form, so famous and so honored, is continually rendered less clear by the discourse of critics, the chatter of journalists, and the plays of even skilled dramatists. In writing of another dramatic form, and one which until now has not even been given a name, I have not, to be sure, been comprehensive, nor do I think I have said the last word.

I do not ask to be listened to, even if wrong, on the ground that my way of being wrong is interesting or idiosyncratic. I claim to be right. If I did not claim this, I should not bother people with my views. But I concede that these views do not cover the whole field of drama, nor have they been focused on all the existing plays of the type I have designated.

The book is composed of pieces written independently. I hope it will be found fundamentally coherent, though I cannot claim that it is systematic. Moreover, in the last section entitled "Relevancies" I have turned aside from the two main themes of the book, tragedy and metatheatre, to deal with matters that are related, although not directly, to my main topics. For instance, I have tried to dispose of an alternative theory of modern drama, Martin Esslin's notion that there is a "theatre of the absurd"; to criticize the enterprise of the Living Theatre, a local institution which has attracted wide interest; and to deny the importance of verse to modern dramatic form.

Perhaps readers should not be encouraged to look for the main assumption of a book in a tiny preface to it. All the same, I am going to state my main assumption here. The studies of dramatic forms which I have made in this book all imply that dramatic forms are related to and take their life from values which are important outside of drama. I am not a formalist. Formalists, I think, are too interested in form as such to really understand it.

LIONEL ABEL

The author wishes to thank *Commentary, Partisan Review,* and *The New Leader* for permission to use some of the pieces in this book.

Contents

TRAGEDY

Daemons, True and False

SOPHOCLES, IN *King Oedipus* and *Oedipus at Colonnus,* set forth the two essential movements of tragedy: in the first play about Oedipus, the protagonist is destroyed; in the second play, having lived through tragic destruction, he becomes divine, a daemon.

Perhaps the best way to understand these different movements is to consider briefly that human fault which, according to Greek thinking, makes tragedy possible: *hubris.* Without *hubris* no character is likely to be destroyed in a tragedy; without being destroyed, no character in a tragedy can become divine, that is to say, a daemon. Thus *hubris* is ambiguous. It can lead to destruction; it can also lead to what, for the Greek mind at least, amounts to something like grace.

Some scholars have insisted that *hubris,* the main tragic fault, is the fault of insolence. On the other hand, Professor Whitman, in his recent book on Sophocles, has tried to demolish the very notion of *hubris.* According to Professor Whitman, the heroes and heroines of Sophocles are motivated not by *hubris,* negative at best, but by *arete,* which is positive and good; for *arete* is the feeling of obligation to the form of one's own virtue. But neither Whitman, who denies that the protagonist of tragedy is guilty of *hubris,* nor those who affirm he is, have understood *hubris,* I think, in all its ambiguities.

Is *hubris* insolence? Simply that? A case could be made out for such a view. But *hubris,* so understood, would throw little light on the movement of Sophocles' plays, or on the way he conceived his heroes and heroines. I suggest that *hubris* is not insolence, and that if a character acts as if he had already undergone tragedy, when in fact tragedy is awaiting him, he is guilty of *hubris.* On the other hand, to have undergone tragedy, to have been destroyed, and yet to live on is to become capable of daemonic power. The character who acts as if he or she had the power of a daemon will be destroyed; after such destruction may come daemonic powers. *Hubris,* then, is a claim to a certain kind of divinity which may or may not be granted.

Not that the protagonist of a tragedy is willing to undergo destruction in order to become a daemon. On the contrary, the tragic protagonist hopes to achieve other and more human ends. But he acts as if he were invulnerable. This fiction leads him to destruction.

In the first Oedipus play of Sophocles we see a perfect example of *hubris.* Oedipus announces that he will find and punish the murderer of Laius. He persists, although advised not to, until he discovers that he himself is the murderer he has sworn to punish, and that the murdered man is his own father. This knowledge destroys him. He blinds and exiles himself. But he does not die.

In Sophocles' second play about Oedipus, the former king, now a blind beggar led by his daughter, having survived tragedy, has become a daemon. Two cities want his body when he dies, for according to the decree of Apollo the city where Oedipus is buried will be blessed. Moreover Oedipus, who has killed his father and paid for that act, feels powerful enough to curse his two sons and doom them both to die, by each other's hand. (Yet Sophocles, wanting to preserve some element of human freedom even in the strictest chain of causality, makes it clear that after Oedipus has cursed his sons they are not necessarily doomed to kill each other; this will happen only if Polynices insists on leading his army against Thebes; if he does insist, however, he will die, as will his brother Eteocles.)

The power shown by a character already destroyed by tragedy is just as tragic, from our reading of *Oedipus at Colonnus,* as the weakness of a character who thinks himself all-powerful and is destroyed tragically. The two plays of Sophocles complement each other and cover the whole domain of tragedy.

What happens when a true daemon encounters a false daemon? This is the subject of Sophocles' *Antigone.*

It has been said that the main characters in the tragedy, Antigone and Creon, are both right—Antigone because she represents the gods of the family, or, if one is an idealist, the laws beyond the gods; Creon because he represents the gods of the State. Such was the view of Hegel, who took *Antigone* to be the most perfect expression of Greek tragedy.

But it is not the case that Antigone and Creon are equally right in their claims. True, Creon appears to be right at certain moments, but only before the entrance of Tiresias; after that, not only is he clearly wrong but, according to Tiresias, the object of the gods' hatred. He has done something cosmically wrong, contravening the order of nature and society: he has buried a living person and refused to bury a dead man. Yet Creon would not be as wrong as he is at the moment Tiresias denounces him if Antigone had not possessed the strength to defy the State's edict. Her *strength* makes Creon a criminal. Had she yielded to his decree, he would have been in error, no doubt, but not totally.

So it is simply not true that Antigone and Creon are ethically equal. Because Hegel thought they were he invented his altogether incorrect—though original and interesting—theory of tragedy, which he took to be a conflict between two equal institutions, the State and the family.

For anyone who has seen a good performance of Sophocles' *Antigone,* it becomes clear that Antigone is right but that the pathetic character in the play is Creon. And to say that Antigone is right is to say much more than that she is right ethically or that the family is more important than the State.

Even if Sophocles thought that the family was more important than the State—which I doubt—it would not be sufficient to account for the rightness of Antigone against Creon. As a matter of fact, Hegel may have been perfectly correct in concluding that an Athenian dramatist would necessarily place the State and the family on equal ethical terms. Still, Antigone and Creon do not contend as equals. Nor does the inequality between them derive from Antigone's superior ethical and religious views. Antigone's superiority to Creon is that she is a true daemon, and he a false one.

This superiority of Antigone, not only to Creon but to

everyone else in the play, is shown in the very first scene, when she proposes to her sister Ismene that they bury their brother Polynices in defiance of Creon's edict. Ismene refuses. How can they, weak as they are, fight against the State? Antigone replies with great harshness that she can and shall, and that she no longer desires her sister's assistance. She will herself bury her brother's body and fight the State as best she can, without help from anyone. She talks with daemonic strength and assurance.

Is Creon a daemon? When he appears, his first statement is an attempt to convince the Chorus that he will stop at nothing to punish whoever, in defiance of his order, does honor to the body of the dead traitor, Polynices. "Why strike a dead man?" the Chorus asks. Creon replies that two brothers are dead, one a hero defending his city, the other a traitor who sought to conquer it. The state must distinguish between the two corpses, and the only way to show contempt for the traitor is to leave his body unburied. Moreover, asserts Creon, the State is so dear to him that in its name he would disregard any tie of friendship or family. For him, he says, the State is everything.

In making this assertion Creon is deceiving himself, for he does care for his son Haemon, who is in love with Antigone. Creon, in speaking as he does to the Chorus, Antigone, and Haemon, speaks as if he were invulnerable to feeling. The strange thing is that Antigone, who speaks in the name of feeling, is invulnerable to any feeling for Haemon, Ismene, or the State. Antigone is truly daemonic, Creon falsely so; she can die. Is she not the daughter of Oedipus and part of his tragedy? Did she not share his exile? Ismene did not. But Creon cannot hear that his son is dead and his wife a suicide without begging to be destroyed. He has already been destroyed, having acted as if he were invulnerable.

II

What happens when two true daemons encounter each other? In *Macbeth*, Shakespeare's one real tragedy in my view, the dramatist pitted Macbeth first against his own wife, a false daemon, and finally against Macduff, a true daemon, made such by Macbeth himself through the murder of Macduff's wife and children.

This play of Shakespeare's is, unhappily, most misunderstood, even by the best critics. T. S. Eliot, so perceptive in his comments on many other Shakespeare plays, writes of *Macbeth* as if it were merely a study of "habituation to evil," a dramatic proof, simply, that, having done evil, one is forced to do it again and again.

> The awful daring of a moment's surrender
> which an age of prudence can never retract.

These lines from Eliot's own verse express sad but not tragic thinking. What about the awful daring of a moment's surrender which places the one who surrenders at a point where he never has to be prudent again? This moment Shakespeare dramatized in *Macbeth*.

Bradley remarked that *Macbeth* is the most rapid of Shakespeare's tragedies. Like the Greek tragedies but unlike Shakespeare's other great plays, it has no subplot. At the opening, Macbeth encounters the witches, who promise that he will be thane of Cawdor, a higher rank than the thaneship he holds, and that finally he will be King. Immediately afterward he discovers that the thane of Cawdor is to be executed for treason and that he, Macbeth, who fought valorously and loyally for Duncan, is to be made Cawdor, just as the witches had prophesied. Were the witches to be taken at their word? Could Macbeth aspire to be King, too? However, there is one ominous aspect to the accession of Macbeth to the dead Cawdor's position. Apparently Cawdor, when executed, conducted himself bravely, and someone says of him: "Nothing became him in life like his leaving of it." The same can be said, at the play's end, of Macbeth.

Lady Macbeth, informed by her husband of his promotion and of the promises of the witches, and informed, too, that the Scottish King is coming to visit their castle, determines to help Macbeth help fate: She is for murdering the King in their own castle the first night he stays there as a guest. Macbeth is full of doubts and moral questions. He argues with her:

> I dare do all that may become a man;
> Who dares do more is none.

Lady Macbeth has already replied by denying her woman-
hood. Before Macbeth arrived at their castle, she had prayed
to be unsexed. In a way, her prayer is to become a witch,
like the Weird Sisters who have stimulated Macbeth's am-
bition. She affirms that she would pluck her own child from
her breast and dash its brains out, rather than see Macbeth
unable to act at the moment when action can mean the
greatest reward of all.

When it comes to action, though, it is Macbeth himself
who does the killing, which Lady Macbeth would not have
been able to do. As she herself admits, the old King reminds
her of her father. At the outset, then, it is Lady Macbeth
who wants to go beyond the human, but cannot. She will
never become a daemon, although her famous speech asking to be unsexed is in fact a prayer to become one. After
the murder of the King, Banquo, and Macduff's wife and
children, Lady Macbeth gives way to madness. Macbeth,
reluctant at first to kill his sovereign and full of guilt after
he has had his old friend Banquo slain, is able to live on
from murder to murder, feeling their horror to the full,
yet never giving way inwardly. When told that Lady Macbeth has died, he can say about life:

> . . . It is a tale
> Told by an idiot, full of sound and fury,
> Signifying nothing

and yet go on living, fighting to the last. The witches of
course have promised him a certain immunity. They have
told him that his life would be safe until Birnam Wood
came to Dunsinane, or until he encountered a man not born
of woman. When the army led by Malcolm and Macduff
approaches, each soldier carrying a branch from the trees
of Birnam Wood, Macbeth begins to suspect that the
promises of the Weird Sisters are mere quibbles. Finally
he encounters Macduff and tells him he has no chance to
win: Macbeth cannot be slain by any man born of woman.
Macduff then reveals that he was "from my mother's womb

untimely ripped." The last protection Macbeth could count on has failed him. He is by now a daemon, beyond other men. But his enemy now is also a daemon, become so, as I have said, through the action of Macbeth himself, who had had Macduff's wife and all of his children killed. In the wonderful scene when Macduff is told of what happened to his family, that his wife and all his children are dead, he asks,

Did you say all?

Perhaps if one of his children had been spared, Macduff would not have been capable of facing Macbeth. I suggest that Shakespeare might even have been pointing to the main meaning of the play, in making Macduff stress the word *all*.

And now Macbeth has no special or peculiar defense against the adversary he has made equal to him. But Macbeth's last words, to Macduff, are beyond hope or despair:

> Though Birnam Wood be come to Dunsinane,
> And thou oppos'd, being of no woman born,
> Yet I will try the last.

These are not the words of a man, but of a daemon, become more than man through tragedy. In a way the Weird Sisters have kept their word to Macbeth. He is elevated now beyond any human station. He has dared "do more than may become a man" and he is more than a man at his death.

Macbeth and Macduff are the only true daemons Shakespeare was able to set successfully on the stage. He tried in other plays to make other characters daemonic; he did not succeed. Is this because the supernatural has to be suggested for a daemon to appear convincing? Were Shakespeare's other intended tragedies too naturalistic? I would venture to answer these questions with a very definite yes, but I do not want to argue for my conviction on this matter here. I should like, though, to call attention to Shakespeare's signal failure to make King Lear daemonic.

Lear has endured the ingratitude and spite of his daughters, the insults of subaltern characters, the ridicule of his fool, the wise scolding of his loyal friend Kent, and the fury of the storm; he has been cast out, humiliated; he is weary, weak, old, drenched; there is no comfort for him anywhere or in anyone; his thought reaches toward madness. Should he not, having undergone all that, become all-powerful after having been all-weak? This is what we want and expect, after the storm scene.

But instead of becoming daemonic, Lear goes mad. Shakespeare, whose intuitive understanding of dramatic law was so profound, must have sensed that madness was not quite right or appropriate to the tragic rhythm he wanted in this play. Shakespeare does make Lear speak marvelously —in a philosophic sense about order and anarchy, justice and injustice, lechery and virtue—but Lear's daemonic philosophizings do not suffice to make the man a daemon. Finally Shakespeare resorts to a kind of symbolism: Lear appears crowned with flowers, suggesting Christ. But to suggest the Christian God in some vague sense, is not the same as to become *dramatically* divine through suffering. Lear, crowned with flowers, is utterly weak and defenseless. He cannot protect Cordelia. She is killed and he dies unable to avenge her. The movement of the play carries him to ultimate weakness, and there is no corresponding movement lifting him toward absolute strength.

Yet the whole beauty and force and power of the play, despite its fundamental disorder, lies in the suggestion that Lear could or might be daemonic. Lear symbolizes daemonism with his inspired utterances, violent gestures, scolding of the storm, with his nakedness and his crown of flowers. This king Shakespeare tried to make divine but could not. Lear is neither a true nor a false daemon: he is just a human being whose sufferings make him potentially daemonic. This is not because of a fault in Lear, but because of some lack in the play in which Shakespeare placed him. Lear has as much wit, natural pride, dignity, and power as Oedipus of *Oedipus at Colonnus,* but he cannot move us as the Oedipus of that play does. For Oedipus, through his suffering, has acquired the ultimate power great suffering can give. Lear goes from his initial power to lesser and lesser power until the end. He becomes only symbolically strong; but this symbolism betrays the faultiness—in dramatic terms—of Shakespeare's tragedy.

Is there such a thing as a bad daemon? Can anyone who has gone through tragedy want to do evil? In my opinion —and one can only guess here—anyone who has gone through tragedy is beyond the pettiness implied by the desire to hurt others. An evil daemon would have to be someone made invulnerable to suffering by tragedy yet interested in doing evil.

To be convinced that an evil daemon exists, we would have to see on the stage someone who has gone through what Macbeth, Oedipus, or Lear has endured, and still wants to do evil. There is no such dramatic character. Yet there almost is. In Shakespeare's *Richard III,* when Richard describes his body as "a chaos or an unlicked bear whelp," we know he has suffered greatly. Still Richard is never great in defeat; he is brilliant in victory; he does not understand defeat, only victory over others. He is intellectually superior to all of his opponents, stronger and more calculating, with more will, more consciousness, and fewer or no scruples. But he is not beyond his opponents; he is on the same plane as they are.

What about Iago? He seems daemonic enough; Coleridge characterized him as having a "motiveless malignity." Certainly he has more force than any other character in *Othello.* But is he a true daemon? Shakespeare seems to have wanted to present him as such, and Iago's last words when he is caught are strangely like Hamlet's. Hamlet says "the rest is silence." Iago, when asked why he plotted against Othello and Desdemona, says, "I shall never more speak word." But yet we feel that Iago, the intriguer, despite his last words, has not become indifferent to success or failure.

If, as Kant has it, there is radical evil in the universe, then a bad daemon ought to be possible. Rational thought has to deny this, and dramatic thinking has never been able to present a daemonic devil on the stage. The Mephistopheles of Goethe's *Faust* is the devil only if we assume him to have magical power. The dramatic character he reveals is that of a very enlightened and intelligent scoundrel. This is no superman.

Very probably there must be something ideal about the

structure of the world in which tragedy is possible. If the worst were the strongest, or, to use Claudel's term, the "surest," tragedy would be inconceivable. One cannot feel the power of loss when there is nothing significant to lose. Thus it is that Greek taste, which was most assured on this matter, excluded villains from the tragic universe. Shakespeare's taste was not as good, and in trying to make of *Lear* a tragedy he admitted Edmund, Goneril, and Regan into the action, giving them the most dynamic roles, too. Perhaps this is why he was unable to make Lear daemonic, as the play required.

Whether or not the Devil exists is a metaphysical question which cannot be answered here. Dramatically, though, it may be said that the Devil does not exist, for in a stage work the Devil's strength, whatever it be, will always appear more human and less forceful than the daemonic power which goes with absolute weakness.

The Fate of Athaliah—and Racine

I

A FIGURE shaped to the purpose of tragedy—such is Athaliah, Queen of Judah, daughter of Ahab and Jezebel, even as she appears, set violent before us, strictly judged and summarily disposed of, in the Second Book of Kings.*

A faithful daughter and a monstrous grandmother, Athaliah fell victim to the only grandson whom she had failed to kill. Except for this grandson, Joash, and her father, Ahab, every male member of Athaliah's immediate family was either destroyed by God or slain by her. God, having avenged Himself on Athaliah's mother, Jezebel, encompassed the ruin of Athaliah's brothers, of her husband, Joram, and of all her sons, including Ahaziah, King of Judah. The Lord, not satisfied with vengeance on Jezebel,

* Athaliah's story is recounted with like brevity in the Second Book of Chronicles.

was interested, it seems, in wiping out the posterity of
Ahab,* who were an offense to Him. But Athaliah, equal
to her terrible Opponent, was ready to match Him murder
for murder, life for life. She undertook to wipe out the
posterity of David, though this meant slaughtering her own
grandsons. In their veins the blood of David mingled with
the blood of Ahab. To extirpate the one race meant to
sacrifice the other. Before this atrocity, Athaliah, headlong
and sanguinary, did not flinch. At the eleventh hour it was
God who did. (From a theological view, had He not
wavered, humanity would have lost. Was not the promised
Messiah ordained to come from David's seed?) Suddenly
the Lord bethought Him that He would have to save some
of the blood of Ahab in order not to lose all of David's.
Thus, from the cruel Queen's assault upon her grandsons,
the infant Joash was by miracle preserved. The boy,
found and hidden by Jehosheba, wife to the High Priest
Jehoiada, was raised secretly by them, and in time was
revealed to the people as David's descendant. After a
palace revolution Joash assumed the throne. His grandmother was put to the sword.

These facts are sufficient to justify our judgment that
Athaliah is tragic—to the most eminent degree. And in
how many meanings of the word! First, for the greatness
of her Opponent (could there be a greater?); then, for
being even more uncompromising than He, and again, for
the grandeur of the aim which she refused to compromise.
And when we think about that aim, we see that she is
tragic in still another and—to a modern mind—especially
interesting sense: her aim was precisely tragedy; her purpose was to bring the epic history of the Jews to a bloody
close. If it was God who began the tragedy, it was Athaliah
who continued it from the point where He left off, so that
He was finally forced to intervene and prevent her from
accomplishing what had originally been His own design.
Thus Athaliah's action, until the very end, is indistinguish-

---

* Ahab appears to have escaped God's wrath, which is undoubtedly why God was so vengeful toward his descendants.
In any case, Ahab's escape from God's anger seems to have
made his name the appropriate one for Herman Melville's
impious hero in *Moby Dick*.

able from God's. We may even say that God realized His
vengeance by means of her: in her appeared the rigor He
Himself had to renounce. So if the Queen was accursed,
all of her acts were sacred.

II

Seen thus, Athaliah surely merits our respect; yet she does
not appear to have greatly impressed the writers of the Book
of Kings (or Chronicles). It is not surprising that this rebel
against God elicited little admiration from those who wrote
the Scriptures; but one wonders that the writers did not
take some lyrical note of the Queen's quality. They had,
after all, written wonderfully of her scarcely better mother,
Jezebel, fashioning in their best rhythms an imperishable
image of flaming iniquity. Jezebel's fate is prophesied: "In
the portion of Jezreel shall the dogs eat the flesh of Jezebel,
and the body of Jezebel shall be as dung on the face of
the field in the portion of Jezreel, so that they shall not
say 'This is Jezebel.' " This marvelous malediction—pro-
nounced by a prophet with the oddly delightful name of
Elijah the Tishbite—has surely helped to make Jezebel
remembered. But Athaliah is scarcely depicted in the Book
of Kings. We hear nothing that she says; she is never
characterized; only her deeds are told. The only poetry she
has comes from the facts of her story. The figure of
Athaliah, as the Bible presents her, is purely, exclusively
tragic. And for centuries the Queen remained imaginatively, poetically unknown. But in 1691, Jean Racine presented *Athalie,** his last and one of his most original tragedies, at Saint-Cyr. This play may be said to do more than
remedy the neglect suffered by the Queen at the hands of

---

* Georges Mongredian, in his book *Athalie,* claims there were
no literary sources for Racine's play besides the Old Testament.
But Professor Meyer Schapiro has shown me a brief text on
Athaliah in Boccaccio's book on the misfortunes of celebrated
persons. Translated into French, Boccaccio's work appeared
with a medallion of Athaliah by Fouquet. Racine must have
read the book. Boccaccio's book contains texts on two other
famous persons treated by Racine: Agrippina and Berenice.
However, the text of Boccaccio on Athaliah is quite brief, not
especially penetrating, and tells us little not already known from
the Bible.

the writers of Kings and Chronicles. Sainte-Beuve called
Athalie "as beautiful as *King Oedipus,* and with the true
God to boot." Voltaire judged it "the masterpiece of the
human mind."

III

Athaliah's epiphany, so long delayed, so perfect when
it came, required, of course, some help from chance. I shall
review briefly the favoring, well-known circumstances. Jean
Racine, brought up at Port Royal, learned the Greek
classics together with the Bible; his understanding of the
Greek conception of fate blended with his awe at the implacable acts of the Old Testament God. Evidently the
writing of *Athalie* required a sensibility formed both by
Jansenism and the Greek dramatists; the very same sensibility, though, was essential for the writing of *Phèdre.* It
would seem to me, too, that simply to compare Racine the
orphan, brought up by the nuns at Port Royal, and the
grandson of Athaliah, raised by the High Priest, Jehoiada,
can tell us little about *Athalie* or the likelihood that Racine
would write it. Let us note, instead, everything that might
have prevented him from writing that play.

Racine began his career as a court poet. His subjects
were taken from Roman history and Greek mythology,
and while he was, no doubt, influenced in his bent for
tragedy by the religious education he had received at Port
Royal, still the themes of his first plays had been almost
exclusively erotic. Nothing surprising in this: the new
young court of Louis XIV was almost exclusively interested
in erotic relations. However, in 1677, *Phèdre* failed, as the
result of an intrigue against Racine. The dramatist had
considered this play his greatest work. His judgment may
be questioned; but certainly *Phèdre* contains the most wonderful poetry Racine was capable of writing. Had the play
succeeded, it is likely that Racine would have continued
to make dramatic poetry out of Greek and Roman stories;
we might have had an *Alceste* by him and an *Iphigénie en
Tauride.* We might not have had *Esther* or *Athalie.* But
Phèdre failed, and Racine stopped writing plays, embarking
on his new career as court memorialist. Twelve years later
Madame de Maintenon asked him to write a dramatic

poem to be played by the girls of Saint-Cyr. She specified that the work should be without erotic interest. Racine hesitated. Madame de Quellus, who knew of the affair, notes in her memoirs: "He wanted to please Madame de Maintenon. Refusal was impossible for a courtier, but the commission was a delicate one for a man who had a great reputation to maintain and who, while he had abandoned writing for the theatre, nevertheless did not want to diminish the reputation his works had gained." We know that Boileau himself advised Racine against accepting. But Racine accepted, and *Esther* was presented before the King and court at Saint-Cyr in 1689. The play was a success and Madame de Maintenon requested another. Racine wrote *Athalie*. It was produced in 1691, and did not find favor; in fact, Louis XIV is said to have left in a rage. Racine wrote no more plays. If *Esther* had not succeeded and if *Phèdre* had not failed, Racine would probably not have written *Athalie*.

Yet how could he not have written *Athalie?* What, from the facts, seems like a wonderfully lucky chance, appears as indispensable and necessary when we take into account Racine's special qualities as a writer of tragedy, and the value of his last work. Of all the authors of tragedy since Aeschylus, Racine, by temperament, training, and resolve, was probably the most gifted for making murder meaningful on the stage. Athaliah, in Racine's last play, is put to death more perfectly than any character in all dramatic literature, and I do not exclude the deaths of Agamemnon and Clytemnestra in the *Orestiae,* the death of King Pentheus in the *Bacchae,* the deaths of Anthony and Cleopatra, and of Macbeth. Yet before he wrote *Athalie*, Racine, with some six or seven dramatic masterpieces behind him, had not yet killed anyone on the stage adequately, let alone perfectly.

IV

Thierry Maulnier and Jean Giraudoux have underscored Racine's capacities as a killer of his characters; but they never saw how dependent this estimate of him is on what he achieved in his last work. Certainly their estimate is not justified by his prior works alone.

Andromaque, for example—which French critics from
La Harpe to Maulnier have regarded as a tragedy—is far
too psychological and romantic a melodrama for the deaths
of two of its main characters, at the climax, to strike us
tragically. The loves of Orestes for Hermione, of Hermione
for Pyrrhus, and of Pyrrhus for Andromache, are frankly
presented by Racine himself as sentiments not quite worthy
of persons of their rank and station. In fact, Racine's judgment of the sentiments of his own characters does not differ
much from that of his rival, Corneille, who disliked *Andromaque,* nor from that of Madame de Sévigné, who liked
it, but thought that it fell short of the sublimity Corneille
had taught the French court to admire. The passions of
Pyrrhus, Orestes, and Hermione are not to be admired, nor
did Racine intend them to be.

Let us note, though, that these three characters are the
children of the great figures whose exploits Homer had
celebrated: Orestes is the son of Agamemnon; Pyrrhus the
son of Achilles; Hermione the daughter of Helen. The one
character in the drama who comes directly from Homer's
Iliad is Andromache, the widow of Hector. Now her feeling
for her dead husband *is* sublime. Andromache's passion,
which we cannot but admire, is more natural than that exhibited by any character in any play by Corneille. She is
the prisoner of Pyrrhus, Achilles' son. Achilles had killed
her husband, and Pyrrhus, conqueror of Troy, had slain her
father and brothers. Now Pyrrhus, who is in love with her,
has the power of life and death over her son by Hector, the
boy Astyanax:

So young, so to be pitied, but yet the one link remaining between any still living Trojan and all the kings dead and buried
under the ruins of Troy.*

If Andromache refuses Pyrrhus she will betray Hector,
for Pyrrhus will kill Hector's son and heir. But if she ac-

---

* *Astyanax, d'Hector jeune et malheureux fils,*
    Reste de tant de rois sous Troie ensevelis.

(*Andromaque:* Act I, scene 1); from my own translation of the
play, published in *The Genius of the French Theater,* edited by
Albert Bermel (Mentor Book). All following translations from
Racine in this text are also mine.

cepts Pyrrhus' love in order to save Hector's son, she will
be unfaithful to Hector. From this tragic dilemma no happy
outcome is conceivable, except by chance. Racine in his
play provided just that chance. The tragically conceived
Andromache does not die, is not forced to marry Pyrrhus,
and yet saves her son. The romantically conceived Pyrrhus
dies at the hand of Orestes, and the equally romantic (and
very modern) Hermione takes her own life. Certainly
there is a tragic tonality in the play: the events express the
just revenge of Troy on Greece for the brutal excesses of
the Greek victors; yet the one really tragic figure succeeds,
and comes through the action safely. The pathetic, somewhat comical and modernly complicated characters are ill-
starred, and fail or die. This is an extraordinary work; it is
not a true tragedy.

In *Bajazet*, which, too, has been called a tragedy, all
the principal characters are killed at the end, strangled by
the gigantic Negro executioner in the harem where the
drama takes place. There are many deaths, but after reading
and rereading the play, and after having seen it on the
stage, one must agree with the seventeenth-century judgment: there is no reason for so much butchery. Racine, in
this play, does demonstrate his temperament for killing,
but he does not reveal himself as one with the *right* to kill,
which, on the stage, means the ability to inflict death
tragically.

No, *Bajazet* is no tragedy. Roxanne, the favorite of the
absent Sultan, whom she is planning to depose, orders Bajazet to marry her. He, being in love with Atalide, after
much hesitation, finally refuses. Roxanne brutally sends him
to the strangler. But had Bajazet accepted Roxanne's offer
of love, his end would have been the same, for Acomat,
the Sultan's grand vizier, returning to take charge of the
harem, would certainly have meted out the same fate to
Bajazet that he does to Roxanne. Moreover, there is something commonplace in Bajazet's character, and something
comical about his trying to be heroically true to his senti-
ment for one woman while living in a harem.

One character is indeed touched by tragedy: Atalide.
She loves Bajazet, and knowing Roxanne will be unmerci-
ful if he refuses her, implores him to accept her rival's

offer. The scene in which she makes this plea is touching and beautiful, perhaps all the more so because Atalide, urging her own lover to be unfaithful to her, is realistic, not idealistic. Bajazet, as I have already noted, in preferring death to infidelity, seems, given the circumstances, not to know where he is. The movement of the play is pure melodrama; nothing great is at issue, and Bajazet is not really a romantic lover. Some French critics have called him a Christian gentleman who had wandered by chance into a harem; this judgment, far from justifying the play, makes it seem, for all its brilliance, somewhat absurd.

Neither *Britannicus* nor *Mithridate* need be considered at length. In the latter play there is a lovely woman, Monine, whom Voltaire thought a great creation. With her, he said, Racine "introduced taste into heroism." It is a fine remark. Yet Voltaire did not consider the play a tragedy. How could he have? It ends happily. Voltaire, however, did think *Britannicus* a tragedy. In this drama, Nero begins his career as a monster by killing his half-brother, Britannicus, in order to defeat the political intrigues of his mother, Agrippina. Evil is triumphant in the beautifully structured and eloquent drama. The true antagonists are Nero and Agrippina, between whom there is no moral issue, only a question of power. The young Britannicus and Junie, who love each other, are children. Whether they live or die, the fate of Rome will be unaltered. Britannicus is killed and Junie escapes from Nero by becoming a vestal virgin. Rome will be controlled by one or the other of the two evil persons in the drama, and it is hardly thinkable that Rome under Agrippina would be different from Rome under Nero. How can the death of Britannicus affect us tragically, then? The play, in its psychology and rhetoric, is "for connoisseurs," as Voltaire noted, but certainly not for connoisseurs of tragedy.

Consider Racine's first and probably most perfect tragedy, *Bérénice*. This is one of the most simply constructed and beautiful plays ever written. It is tragic throughout, yet it does not end with the death of its protagonists, Titus, Emperor of Rome, and Berenice, the Jewish queen who loves him and is loved by him. They are unable to marry because Roman republican law, surviving under the Empire, forbids an emperor to marry a queen. As long as Augustus, the father of Titus, lived, Titus and Berenice expected to marry. When the play begins, Augustus has just died, and Titus realizes at last that he cannot defy the law of the state over which he hopes to rule. Titus sends Antiochus, a visiting king from the East, who also is in love with Berenice, to inform her that the new Emperor of Rome cannot marry her. Antiochus is eager to bear the message; he sees a chance to plead his own case. But when he has told Berenice of the decision of Titus, she peremptorily dismisses him, forbidding him even to see her again. Antiochus is almost comical in this scene, and would indeed be, if Racine, with extraordinary finesse, had not saved him for tragedy by endowing him with a wonderful discretion. Racine also gave him one of his greatest, saddest, and most admired lines:

What shape could my grief take in the all-vacant East?*

At last Berenice confronts Titus, and he tells her in his own words that he cannot marry her. Is he not the Emperor? she wants to know. He is the Emperor, and that is why he cannot obey his heart. Titus even considers giving up his empire for Berenice, but would she love him if he were not the Emperor of Rome? They part forever, and the last word of the play, spoken by Antiochus, is "alas."

The movement of this play has the sureness of the very greatest tragedies. The mechanism is flawless. Rome, which decrees the separation of the lovers, is identical with the civilized world. It is the world at its best which denies what is best in the lovers: their feeling for each other. In the end they both recognize this. All the same, they choose to live. Moreover, the plot allows them to live, and we do not have to believe completely their protests that they would rather die than part. Racine himself, feeling that the absence of death from his play might be regarded as a fault, argued in his preface to it that death is not essential in tragedy. His argument is interesting:

---

* *Dans l'Orient désert quel devint mon ennui!*
             (*Bérénice:* Act I, scene 4)

I grant that I did not push Berenice to the point of a suicide like Dido's, for Berenice was not bound as irrevocably to Titus as Dido to Aeneas; thus she was not obliged, like Dido, to refuse to live at all. Nevertheless, her final farewell to Titus, and her struggles to give him up, are not, I think, the least tragic moments of my play; I shall even go so far as to say that the emotion which the play had already excited is intensified in these moments. Blood and corpses are, after all, not essential to tragedy: enough if the action be great, the characters heroic, their emotions real; enough if the work provokes by its every detail, that majestic sadness wherein lies the whole pleasure of tragedy.

Racine's argument for not having pushed Berenice to the point of a death like Dido's is not strong. It is conventional and one may doubt that it was written with full conviction. What is interesting about the passage—aside from the beautiful phrase explaining "the whole pleasure of tragedy" —is the fact that Racine, so praised as an *ange extermina- teur* (angel of death), should here be arguing that death is not essential to the main purpose of the tragic poet.

In his *Iphigénie à Aulis,* there is death, blood is shed, but not the blood of Iphigenia. Death is meted out to Eriphilia, substituted at the last moment on the sacrificial altar for Iphigenia, and Eriphilia is too calculating and vicious for her death to touch us. As Racine noted in his preface, he chose that variant of the Greek story in which the daughter of Theseus and Helen is sacrificed, suffering the fate the gods demanded for Iphigenia, the daughter of Agamemnon. Racine argues that it would have been in bad taste to have Iphigenia sacrificed, since she was innocent and virtuous. According to Aristotle, he is right, and Racine understood Aristotle better than any other dramatic author of his time. It is, therefore, all the more surprising that Racine did not wish to see that the sacrifice of Eriphilia— in view of her character—was just as contradictory to Aristotle's conception of tragedy as the sacrifice of Iphigenia would have been. For while the Greek philosopher held that the death of a good person is untragic, causing the spectator to suffer too much, he maintained also that the death of a bad person is equally untragic, since it cannot but gladden the one witnessing it. The true tragic emotion is more complicated.

In fact, Racine's whole argument is disingenuous. Iphigenia, though virtuous, could die in a properly Aristotelian tragedy if she were not the protagonist of the play—if, for instance, this role were reserved for her father, Agamemnon, who, in every variant of the story, agrees to her sacrifice so that the winds can blow and the Greek fleet sail. Like Hegel, Kierkegaard understood that the protagonist in any tragedy about the sacrifice of Iphigenia would have to be Agamemnon. And when Kierkegaard resolved to oppose a hero of religion to a hero of tragedy, he elected for Abraham, intent on sacrificing Isaac, as against Agamemnon, prepared to kill his daughter.

The truth is that Racine wanted Iphigenia as his protagonist because he wanted a play with erotic interest. In *Iphigénie à Aulis,* Eriphilia is the rival of Iphigenia for the love of Achilles; Iphigenia gets Achilles and Eriphilia is sacrificed in her place. The winds blow, the ships sail, the evil character has been punished, the good girl saved, and what makes this consummation so utterly untragic is that the army of Agamemnon can now head, without a pang of conscience, for the brutal ten years of carnage on the plains of Troy.

The art of inflicting tragic death on the stage is a difficult one, and even with his ninth play, Racine had not yet mastered it. Did he succeed in *Phèdre?*

This play is considered by most critics to be Racine's greatest. It is his most famous, the one most universally known, and the role of Phaedra is as prized by French actresses as that of Hamlet by actors on the English-speaking stage. I do not wish to examine this judgment here. Surely, the play is great; as certainly, it is faulty. But the point I want to insist on here is that with *Phèdre,* Racine for the first time in his career succeeds in constructing a tragedy that ends with tragic death. *Bérénice,* his first real tragedy, did not.

Yet as has been pointed out by French critics, Phaedra is almost dead at the moment the play begins. She loves her stepson Hippolytus, but she is not reconciled to the sinfulness of an adulterous and incestuous passion; she never forgets that she is the daughter of Pasaphaë, queen of the pure sky, and of Minos, king of Hades, who sits in judg-

ment on the dead. Her first words on her entrance express
her hatred for life and her desire to die:

> No, not another step. I need your arm.
> I can scarcely stand erect. My strength is gone.
> My eyes shut on that sun I have not seen so long.
> My knees give way. Oenone, stay. You be strong.*

Oenone, after long questioning, succeeds in making Phaedra
confess to the cause of her torment and of her desire to die.
When Phaedra finally admits to her passion for Hippolytus,
she does so with a relentless exactitude. There is nothing
comparable to the truthfulness of this confession by any
character in Shakespeare:

The ill, the ache, come from farther off. I was
The bride of Theseus, happy, or without cause
For any unhappiness. My mind was free,
When in Athens I came on my great enemy.
I saw him, I blushed, I paled, incredulous, dazed—
I had not thought I could be so amazed.
I could scarcely see. I could not speak. I stood,
Rigid, frozen, burning, flesh and blood!
I knew then the power of Venus to subjugate
With love whoever has incurred her hate.
She had shown her power. For me to circumvent it!
I built her a temple, richly ornamented.
I ordered sacrifice made. Myself I picked the beasts!
I searched for my lost reason in their flesh.
Weak remedies for love that will not die!
Vainly I lit the altar fires, I
Spoke the name of the Goddess reverently,
But still loved Hippolytus, saw him constantly.

         .   .   .

I avoided him yet found him. Fateful chance!
The son's features were in his father's countenance! . . .
I turned against every throb in me that wooed him
And took heart from a plan: it was to persecute him!

         .   .   .

I demanded his exile and my continual plea
At last banished him to Troezene and far from me.

---

* N'allons point plus avant, demeurons, chère Oenone.
  Je ne me soutiens plus; ma force m'abandonne:
  Mes yeux sont éblouis du jour que je revoi;
  Et mes genoux tremblants se dérobent sous moi.
                              (Phèdre: Act I, scene 3)

I breathed again, Oenone, once again,
My days were guiltless though not without pain.
I tried to be faithful to my marriage vows,
Submissive to my husband, a dutiful spouse.
Vain effort. Cruel stroke! Venus the cause!
I was brought to Troezene, and by Theseus.
I saw Hippolytus. I knew my fate. It was—
It is no fugitive passion to hide, confide, betray!
It's the whole length of Venus, stretched out over her prey!*

Phaedra, resolved to die, is kept alive by the rumor that
Theseus, her husband, is dead, which makes her love for
her stepson, as Oenone interprets it, "not so extraordinary."

---

* *Mon mal vient de plus loin. À peine au fils d'Égée*
Sous ses lois de l'hymen je m'étais engagée,
Mon repos, mon bonheur semblait être affermi;
Athènes me montra mon superbe ennemi:
Je le vis, je rougis, je pâlis à sa vue;
Un trouble s'éleva dans mon âme éperdue;
Mes yeux ne voyaient plus, je ne pouvais parler;
Je sentis tout mon corps et transir et brûler:
Je reconnus Vénus et ses feux redoutables,
D'un sang qu'elle poursuit, tourments inévitables.
Par des voeux assidus je crus les détourner:
Je lui bâtis un temple, et pris soin de l'orner;
De victimes moi-même à toute heure entourée,
Je cherchais dans leurs flancs ma raison égarée:
D'un incurable amour remèdes impuissants!
En vain sur les autels ma main brûlait l'encens:
Quand ma bouche implorait le nom de la déesse,
J'adorais Hippolyte, et, le voyant sans cesse,

. .

Je l'évitais partout. O comble de misère!
Mes yeux le retrouvaient dans les traits de son père.
Contre moi-même enfin j'osai me révolter:
J'excitai mon courage à le persécuter.

. .

Je pressai son exil; et mes cris éternels
L'arrachèrent du sein et des bras paternels.
Je respirais, Oenone; et, depuis son absence,
Mes jours moins agités coulaient dans l'innocence;
Soumise a mon époux, et cachant mes ennuis,
De son fatal hymen je cultivais les fruits.
Vaines précautions! Cruelle destinée!
Par mon époux lui-même à Trézène amenée,
J'ai revu l'ennemi que j'avais éloigné:
Ma blessure trop vive aussitôt a saigné.
Ce n'est plus une ardeur dans mes veines cachée:
C'est Vénus tout entière a sa proie attachée.

(Act I, scene 3)

Brunetière thought the action of the play invalidated by the
fact that it is based on Phaedra's belief in a false rumor.
But surely this is captious criticism. Phaedra wants to believe that Theseus is dead; a woman in her state of mind
would believe such a rumor, especially when it is believed
by others. Why should Brunetière have assumed that characters inflamed by passion generally act on sound assumptions? No, there is no flaw in Phaedra's acceptance of the
report that her husband is dead. Taking counsel from
Oenone, she confesses her passion to Hippolytus. It was not
her intention to do so; she had meant, instead, to proclaim
her continuing love for Theseus. But Phaedra's passion is
more truthful than she wants to be. Her confession, heard
on the stage, has an absolute magic. We see what is most
inward in a character, expressed against the character's
own wish. She says:

Yes, Prince, I long for, yearn for Theseus.
For him, yet not for him. Not as he was

.   .   .

But as he might be, faithful, even fierce,
Young, charming, proud of head, and pure of brow,
As one depicts a god, or as I see you now.
He had your glance, your bearing, turn of phrase,
That proud reserve I see as yours was his
When he strode up our shore, bright, worthy of
The daughters of King Minos, ripe for love.
Where were you then, Hippolytus? Theseus brought with him
All the brave youth of Greece. Why were not you with them?

.   .   .

You might have slain the fabled minotaur,
Conquered the cunning maze of his vast lair.
My sister Ariadne would to you
Have given the fate-spun thread, and brought you through.
No! I would have given it you! Love would have taught me
That the whole circumstance of your victory
Hung on a thread! No, No! I would have gone down into
That labyrinth, shown each twist of it to you,
Myself, not trusting to a thread so easily
Snapped, to bring you safely back to me!
I would have shared the danger that lay hid
In those dark turns, and run the risks you did.

Yes, Phaedra in the labyrinth would go first
To emerge from it with you—or with you be lost!*

Hippolytus is shocked, morally outraged by this avowal;
he is himself in love with Aricia, Theseus' ward. Rebuffed,
Phaedra has to endure, besides, the return of Theseus. She
permits Oenone to tell her husband that his son has made
advances to her. In a great scene, Theseus vents his rage on
Hippolytus and calls on Poseidon to kill the youth. Poseidon obliges: Hippolytus is killed by a monster from the sea,
whereupon Theseus realizes he had never completely believed Phaedra's story. He tells her, not without bitterness,
of his son's death. She admits the truth and dies, a suicide,
offstage.

Why diminish a work so splendid? But why praise, be-

---

* *Oui, prince, je languis, je brûle pour Thésée:*
Je l'aime, non point tel que l'ont vu les enfers,

. . .

Mais fidèle, mais fier, et même un peu farouche,
Charmant, jeune, traînant tous les coeurs après soi,
Tel qu'on dépeint nos dieux, ou tel que je vous voi.
Il avait votre port, vos yeux, votre langage;
Cette noble pudeur colorait son visage,
Lorsque de notre Crète il traversa les flots,
Digne sujet des voeux des filles de Minos.
Que faisiez-vous alors? Pourquoi, sans Hippolyte,
Des héros de la Grèce assembla-t-il l'élite?

. . .

Par vous aurait péri le monstre de la Crète,
Malgré tous les détours de sa vaste retraite:
Pour en développer l'embarras incertain,
Ma soeur du fil fatal eût armé votre main.
Mais non: dans ce dessein je l'aurais devancée;
L'amour m'en eût d'abord inspiré la pensée;
C'est moi, prince, c'est moi dont l'utile secours
Vous eût du labyrinthe enseigné les détours:
Que de soins m'eût coutés cette tête charmante!
Un fil n'eût point assez rassuré votre amante:
Compagne du péril qu'il vous fallait chercher,
Moi-même devant vous j'aurais voulu marcher;
Et Phèdre au labyrinthe avec vous descendue
Se serait avec vous retrouvée ou perdue.

(Act II, scene 5)

yond its evident merit, a work so great? In *Phèdre* Racine
created a true tragedy, and dealt death to two of his main
characters. Nevertheless, the play is not without fault. First
of all, as we have seen, Phaedra *wanted* to die from the beginning. Her death, when it comes, is therefore less pathetic
and less terrible than would be the death of someone who
had all along desired life. Another, very serious fault: the
gods are involved in the action but not in a way that is
clear. As Phaedra says, she is the victim of Aphrodite. And
it is Poseidon who executes on Hippolytus the curse pro-
nounced by Theseus. A god and a goddess are involved, but
there is no logical or ideological relation between them.

In the Euripides play, from which Racine took his story,
Hippolytus was a worshiper of Artemis and Phaedra was
submissive to Aphrodite: Artemis and Aphrodite were at
odds, even at war. Hence, for Euripides, the deaths of
Phaedra and Hippolytus followed from an irreconcilable
dispute between two goddesses, one representing spiritual
power against sex, the other the force of sex as such. Hippolytus refuses Phaedra, not because he loves another woman,
but because he does not and cannot love at all, being vowed
to Artemis. Racine's play is undoubtedly greater than the
play of Euripides; yet its construction is less logical, its
final meaning less clear.

Racine had finally killed a sympathetic character in a
great but faulty tragedy.

v

In a novel, characters can grow old and die; on the stage
a character, whose dying is to interest us, must be put to
death. There is a most interesting recognition of this in
Shakespeare's *Henry IV,* Part II. Henry IV is dying. He has
fallen asleep. Prince Hal enters, thinks his father already
dead, removes the crown from his head, and speaks as if he,
Prince Hal, were already Henry V. Henry IV awakes, accuses Prince Hal of wanting to kill him. In a subsequent
scene we learn that Henry IV has died. The cause of death
is, of course, old age and exhaustion; yet, Henry IV has
been killed symbolically by his son, and thus has had a
proper theatrical end.

The taking of a person's life is the most drastic, the most dramatic act there is. Obviously the most fundamental sanctions are involved. To kill—to destroy a life one has not created—is an *imitatio dei*, even when committed by an atheist. What about the infliction of death on an imaginary person, a fiction, a character in a play?

In my view—I am aware it may strike the reader as a paradox—it is as difficult to justify inflicting death on a character as to justify killing a real person. Perhaps the difficulty will be best understood if one thinks in purely rational terms of passing judgment on another life. One will then realize that no reason is sufficient. Also, there is this fact: The best and most convinced assassins have always been fanatics. Has one the right to kill without being fanatical? And does the dramatist who wants to bring his protagonist to a tragic end also have to be a fanatic is some sense?

In his fine book *Death in the Afternoon,* Hemingway pointed out that the best killers of bulls have never been the best or most skilled matadors. Those bullfighters whom Hemingway most admired as artists, he did not admire most for their manner of killing. On the contrary, he claims, the men who killed best were fairly simple, uncomplicated persons, rather unskilled in the earlier passes, and deft only when it came to the ultimate blow. May this hold, too, for the infliction of death on the stage? Does the great writer of a great tragedy have to be a fairly simple, rather religious fellow, to deliver with sureness the final and culminating stroke?

Or is it sheer skill in dramaturgy which justifies the playwright in putting a character to death when death is required by his plot? Yet Corneille, in so many ways a more skillful playwright than Racine, was inept at inflicting death. In fact, his plays, so well plotted, become disorganized once death occurs. Corneille, the dramatist of the rational will, thought he could clarify everything, but he could not impose death purposefully. Once *Le Cid* has killed the father of Chimène, the play collapses. Chimène, though she loves the man who has killed him, must avenge her father's death. If she does not, she is unworthy to be the wife of Rodrigue, or a heroine of Corneille. On the other hand, Corneille has plotted his play so that Chimène and Rodrigue must marry, and he is unable to resolve this contradiction. Something similar occurs in *Horace*. The younger Horatius has seen his two brothers die at the hands of the three Curiations. He succeeds in killing the three, one of whom is the husband of his sister. She curses her brother and Rome. Whereupon Corneille's hero kills her. This was intended to be an exalted moment, expressing patriotic emotion. But one imagines that Corneille was a bit sickened by his own hero's action. In fact, the old Horatius, the hero's father, does not admire what his son has done. Nor do the Roman leaders, who have the problem of hailing the young Horatius as the savior of Rome, and of justifying his murder of his own sister. The play is never a tragedy, and it ends in what is very close to farce. The hero is acclaimed, but those who applaud him would prefer to try him for murder.

One needs something better than reasons to justify killing. This holds both in real and in imagined action.

What can justify killing on the stage? The feeling that the death of the character is destined. But what is meant by the word *destiny?*

If a rational meaning could be assigned to this term, there would be no such thing as tragedy. Yet how can the term *destiny* be understood, if not rationally?

Francis Bradley and Henri Bergson have pointed out that certain truths appear evident to consciousness when felt with a certain intensity, and that at a lesser intensity, these truths appear as contradictions. Does this notion apply here?

Let us take a play of Shakespeare's, commonly regarded as a tragedy, but in which the death of each significant and appealing character disgusts us with life and with the play, too. In *King Lear,* the deaths of Gloucester, Lear, and Cordelia are all horrible and unjustifiable in aesthetic terms. There are two remarks in *Lear* which relate to destiny, and they contradict each other:

> As flies to wanton boys, are we to th' gods,
> They kill us for their sport.

and

> The gods are just, and of our pleasant vices,
> Make instruments to plague us.

Clearly, these remarks refute each other. The difficulty of
thinking that both are true is the chief problem of Shakespeare's play and prevents it from being a true tragedy. We
cannot accept or be exalted by the deaths of Gloucester,
Cordelia, or Lear himself. There is no destiny in any of
these deaths, for in a true vision of destiny, the contradiction implied by the two views that (1) the gods are wanton
in their treatment of us, and (2) the gods are just in their
treatment of us, would be transcended. The deaths of Lear
and Gloucester seem to follow from the proposition that
the gods are just. The death of Cordelia—which Samuel
Johnson found so objectionable, and which prompted him
to suggest that Shakespeare was never at his best but always
somewhat labored when it came to writing tragedy—seems
to follow from the proposition that we are to the gods like
flies to wanton boys. So that the deaths in *King Lear* follow
from conflicting principles. The work is simply not unified.
And this is one reason it tends to be ineffective on the stage.

Shakespeare did, of course, write *Macbeth*. When he
wrote *King Lear* he did not, I think, have the single vision
which tragedy requires. "Let your eye be single, and your
body will be filled with light." Altered to our purpose, and
addressed to the dramatist, these words of the New Testament would read: Let your eye be single and you will be
able to bring the darkness of death tragically to the stage.

Shakespeare must have felt at some moment in his career
that his interests were too varied, his skepticism too acute,
for him to kill his own characters tragically. Even as the
Duke of Vienna, in *Measure for Measure,* questions his
fitness for punishing his subjects severely, so, I suggest,
Shakespeare questioned his right to kill dramatically. He
did not lack the technical means, to be sure; neither, of
course, did Corneille. But Corneille, great playwright and
poet though he was, did not have the kind of conscience we
have a right to assume Shakespeare had, in giving up tragedy
altogether to create an entirely new kind of drama.

The vision of the tragedian has to be single and simple.
Are we back then with the thought that the tragic artist has
to be an uncomplicated person? Religious if not devout? Or
not unlike those men Hemingway described as the best kill-

ers in the bull ring? Now I would not altogether reject the notion, often held, that the great tragic artists have been religious persons. Dostoyevsky was one of the most complicated of men; perhaps he was not a believer, but certainly he wanted to believe. In his sophistication, he desired to be naïve. Though not a playwright, he was the most dramatic of all novelists—and the most tragic, too. In the *Brothers Karamazov,* Fyodor Karamazov is killed, in fact, by his illegitimate and epileptic son Smerdyakov. The real murderer, of course, is his eldest son Ivan, who has indicated by certain signs—though not in so many words—to Smerdyakov, who admires him, that he, Ivan, would be pleased by the old man's death. Can we say that Ivan killed his father knowingly? We cannot. Can we say he killed his father without knowing? We cannot say that either. The murder of the old Karamazov would have satisfied Aristotle completely. There is nothing more sophisticated in all of ancient or modern dramaturgy. No simple-minded dramatist could have brought off such an effect.

Dostoyevsky was able to feel Fyodor Karamazov's death as wanton and yet as justified. From the outset of the novel, Dostoyevsky had presented Fyodor as hated by his sons— all except the near-saint, Alyosha. The inability of Fyodor's sons to love him doomed him; they would have had to be saints for him not to have been murdered.* Thus his murder is inevitable, and yet his sons are responsible. This seems to us a paradox on reflection, not when we read the *Brothers Karamazov.*

Could Dostoyevsky have so succeeded without being or wanting to be religious? It is doubtful. The desire for a simple faith can be the equivalent, in art at least, of faith itself. Of course, such desire must be genuine. In whom could it be more genuine than in a man tormented by his own complexity? There are many art forms which admit personal complexity as a value. The art of tragedy is quite different. Here complexity is of value only as something to be overcome.

* Alyosha tried to be a saint. His motive may have been to be capable of not killing his father. As matters turned out, though, his interest in the death of the saint, Zossima, prevented him from intervening when he might have saved his father and his brothers.

To avoid any misunderstanding, I wish to make clear that religious belief is not the only kind of belief necessary for that simplification and purity of vision that tragedy requires. Shakespeare, who we tend to think was not religious, did write *Macbeth*. (It is to be noted, though, that this play is the one work of his which projects a necessary order beyond nature's.) Let us put the matter this way: the single view necessary for the tragic poet cannot go without a certain humiliation of the mind, through its acceptance of an inflexible order. Such acceptance was not at all characteristic of Shakespeare. It would be surprising, though, if a man who sympathized with so many postures of consciousness did not, at some time in his career, yield completely to a feeling for fatality.

VI

Racine's life and career can be described as a voluntary yielding to different but always inflexible orders: first to that of the Jansenists, who educated him at Port Royal; then to that of classical Greek tragedy, which he never questioned, though his predecessor in the theatre, Corneille, had; finally to that of the court of Louis XIV. In his excellent book, *Racine and Poetic Tragedy*, Eugene Vinaver writes: "The classical doctrine left the poet the choice of sentiments. Yet, there again Racine forbids himself any boldness and, even in his predilection for certain moral states, does nothing but follow the tastes and tendencies of the century, accommodated to his manner." Vinaver denies that Racine was ever original in his understanding of classical tragedy, but insists that such originality as he shows—and at times this is very marked—was the inevitable result of a good mind yielding to an order which it had merely tried to understand, but not to change.

There was no criticism of the monarchy in Racine's plays—as there is in the works of Molière and Corneille. For most of Racine's life, no doubt, the authority of Louis XIV over Racine was absolute. There is a story that once Racine formulated a program to help the poor and presented it to the King, who is said to have replied: "Just because you're a great poet, don't think you can be a minister." Racine at once put his project aside and is not known to have ever again directly intervened in politics.

How are we to understand this voluntary submission of Racine to religious, classical, and royal authority? It is precisely what makes him exceptional in his own century; and among all the great dramatists of the age, taking into account those of England and Spain as well as of France, Racine was the only one who really tried to be faithful to Aristotle, who never criticized the figure of his king, and who never questioned the religion in which he was indoctrinated as a child. How different he was, not only from his contemporaries, Corneille and Molière, but from Marlowe and Shakespeare, and also from the great Spaniards, Lope de Vega and Calderón!

In the conduct of his life, Racine exhibits a conspicuous purposefulness in advancing his career. Was this dramatist of such poetic purity fundamentally a careerist? Why was there in him no feeling of rebellion, no violence against what was already canonized in religion, politics, and art? I would suggest that Racine concerned himself in the main with the perfect fulfillment of his role, which was to write tragedy. What did not help him in that role was inessential; he must have intuitively felt that the acceptance of the various orders to which he did submit—at times in the interest of his career—was helpful to him in his life task. There is something wonderfully adroit in his inner knowledge of what he needed in order to fulfill himself and to perfect the image we have of him. But we would not have had this image without his last play.

VII

Racine was writing *Athalie.* He had succeeded with *Esther.* His choice of a subject for the new work to be given at Saint-Cyr was the story of Athaliah, who had now found the perfect poet to describe her fate. It is interesting to consider how the two destinies, those of the poet and of the biblical Queen intersect. Athaliah, who had remained fairly insignificant for two thousand years, was now to express herself in one of the greatest tragedies ever written. Racine, who had trained himself to kill tragically on the stage, was for the first time in his career to do so perfectly.

But there were many practical reasons why Racine should not have chosen the subject. Had he been concerned at this point with Louis XIV's opinion of him, and not with faithfully completing his own image, he would surely have elected for some other story. As a courtier, Racine could not but have been aware that Louis XIV, having destroyed Port Royal and imprisoned the leading Jansenists—including the niece of the great Arnaud himself—would not take kindly to a religious play based on the Old Testament, in which a ruling monarch was presented as the enemy of God and overthrown in a revolution led by a priest. Surely Racine knew this. Why then did he risk for the first time in his life the King's displeasure?

Racine was older now. He had a career behind him, one which the court had favored and finally frustrated. Without the support of the court, he would not have written *Andromaque* or *Bérénice*. But it was a court intrigue which had led to the failure of what he considered his greatest work, *Phèdre*. There is something else, too, to be considered. In *Iphigénie à Aulis,* which has been called Racine's "royal tragedy" but is no tragedy at all, Racine, the orphan, had made the villain an orphan, killed her off at the play's close, and thereby destroyed any chance of the work ending tragically. In writing *Athalie*, Racine again chose to deal with an orphan, Joash. This time an orphan would be the hero—backed by the greatest king of all: the Lord. So supported, Racine could risk displeasing Louis XIV. Though he was still submissive to authority, this time Racine would do the one thing which as a writer of tragedy he had thus far left undone.

He also felt free to violate the unities of time and place. In *Esther* he had violated the Aristotelian canon calling for a definite and single place; in *Athalie* both time and place are left undefined. Moreover, as in *Esther*, in *Athalie* he introduced a chorus. What is the reason for the Chorus in his last play?

As Aristotle pointed out, the Chorus must be functional. This is not always the case, even in the works of Sophocles. It is hard to see what function the Chorus has in *The Women of Trachis*. Greek scholars have noted, too, the

purely conventional character of the Chorus in *Philoctetes*.
Apparently Sophocles himself was not incapable of falling
into neoclassicism. But in *Athalie* the Chorus, composed of
young girls, in words taken from the Psalms and put by
Racine into the very purest French, chants a continuous
paean to the majesty, might, and love of the Old Testament
God. Since it is fundamentally God who is the victor over
Athaliah, the verses of the young girls, in adoration of His
glory, have the further purpose of indicating how weak
Athaliah is, how certain her destruction. I have the impression in reading the play that after each chorus—unheard
by Athaliah; she is never present while the Chorus speaks
—she bleeds a little. The verses are like the banderillas
placed in the side of the bull by the matador to weaken and
madden him, preparing him for death.

Athaliah begins to die with the first line of the play ut-
tered by the slightly comical Abner, her military chief, who
is faithful to the true God at the same time that he is loyal
to Athaliah as the legitimate Queen of Judah. Abner does
not suspect that a male descendant of David still lives. And,
although he does not approve Athaliah's worship of Baal,
he will not, for religious reasons, violate the monarchical
principle. His first words are:

I've come to spend a little while with God.*

The dropping in on God by Abner, the main support of
Athaliah, sets the tone for each subsequent happening.
Jehoiada, the High Priest, protests to Abner against the
worship of Baal in the kingdom, which has the Queen's
backing. Abner would like to be indignant too, but does not
think it proper to be critical of his sovereign. He suggests
that the time of miracles is past and brings down on himself a ringing denunciation by the High Priest Jehoiada,
who accuses him of lacking faith. However, the priest knows
that there is a living male descendant of David; Abner does
not. After their interview the High Priest confides to his
wife, Jehosheba, that the time has come to reveal Joash to
the people.

Athaliah has a premonition that Joash exists. She has had

---

* *Oui, je viens dans son temple adorer l'Éternel;*

a dream, which she recounts to her advisers: her mother, Jezebel, has appeared to her

In the dead vast and middle of the night*

and told her that she, too, is about to be overwhelmed by the cruel Old Testament God. Immediately afterward, Athaliah, still dreaming, sees a young boy in priest's dress. The sight of him raises her spirit; she admires his noble and modest air, his gentleness; whereupon the boy plunges a dagger into her breast. She dreams of the boy again and he repeats his action. Deeply troubled on awakening, she thinks of propitiating the God her mother's specter has warned her against. She goes to the temple and sees a young boy in every respect exactly like the boy who has killed her in her dream. Who is this boy? Neither Abner nor Mathan, the High Priest of Baal, know.

Athaliah has already foreseen her own execution. On the point of being destroyed by God, she seems to absorb, by a kind of divine contagion, God's mercy, even as prior to this she had absorbed God's wrath. She goes again to the temple, sees Joash, is again struck by his nobility, pride, and grace; and in an astonishing scene offers to take him to her palace and treat him as her son; she remarks that she has no son and suggests that he might become her heir. The boy rejects her overtures. The extraordinary thing about the scene is the fascination of Athaliah with the boy who, her dream has already informed her, is to be her executioner. Lucien Goldmann interprets Athaliah's attraction to Joash as springing from that uncertainty of judgment noted by most historians in ruling groups about to be overthrown, and I think Goldmann is right in this observation—which points up the extraordinary realism of Racine. All the same, in tragedy, psychological acuteness has mainly a negative value. It aids the dramatist in avoiding error. In other words, Athaliah's weakness for Joash is psychologically plausible, but we are not touched because

* *C'etait dans l'horreur d'une profonde nuit.* (I have, of course, translated this line of Racine by a line of Shakespeare. The verse of Shakespeare is, to be sure, more beautiful and splendid in its suggestion of gloom; yet Racine's line is beautiful also, and aims at the very same effect.)

it is psychologically plausible; we are touched because she loves her grandson, not knowing him to be her grandson, and because his victory over her will mean her death.

She has already died four preparatory deaths by the end of scene VII of the second act: twice in her dream, again when she sees Joash in the temple for the first time, then again in the temple when he repudiates her offer to take him to her palace.

Of course, it is the High Priest who actually plots Athaliah's destruction. After her first two visits to the temple, he induces her to return a third time on the pretext of revealing to her David's "secret treasure." This is not, as Athaliah thinks, gold, but Joash, whose ascent to power will mean her death. She comes with Abner and finds that the assembled Levites have made obeisance to Joash: the High Priest has revealed him as their legitimate king. Abner turns against Athaliah, and her doom is sealed.

Some have questioned whether the High Priest is truly noble. If he is not, then, of course, my claim that Athaliah is killed perfectly, dramatically speaking, would be invalid. Voltaire, having praised the play above all other tragedies, finally elected to attack it as a piece of monumental superstition. He saw at once that the way to attack it was to diminish the character of Jehoiada, whom he called a "bloody, authoritarian priest."

If one has no sympathy for Jehoiada, then *Athalie* is no tragedy. For the form of tragedy requires that we sympathize with both the executioner and the victim. This was suggested by Aristotle when he said that tragedy relieves us of pity and terror, and made still clearer by James Joyce in *The Portrait of the Artist as a Young Man*, when Stephen Daedalus, commenting on Aristotle's *Poetics,* says that in tragedy pity unites us with the sufferer, terror with the cause of suffering. The difficulty of most dramatists trying to produce tragedy is not so much to create a sympathetic victim as to create a sympathetic executioner. After the Greeks, it was probably Racine who did this best, and I have said that he only did it perfectly in his last play, *Athalie.*

But *did* he in *Athalie*? Is Jehoiada ignoble or unsympathetic? One can answer by saying that he does nothing by himself, that all his actions are determined by God. Such was Sainte-Beuve's view:

> The great, or rather the only character in *Athalie*, from its first to its last line, is God. The Lord is there, above the high priest and the boy, and at every moment of this powerful and simple story they are controlled by Him. He Himself remains invisible and immutable; always His presence is felt, although hidden by that Holy of Holies to which Jehoiada goes once each year, always returning stronger because of Him whose strength cannot be measured. This unity, this omnipotence of the Eternal Character, far from destroying the drama, or reducing it to a continuous paean, becomes the dramatic action itself, and rising above all characters in the play, acts on everyone of them. . . .*

Nevertheless, Jehoiada must be justified in his human personality. He is a fanatic, and one can say against him that being fanatical he is incapable of moral experience. Jehoiada has of course dignity, courage, and faith. He belongs to an oppressed minority; and he is an instrument of God's purpose. But these facts are not sufficient, as Racine must have known, to make him sympathetic enough for us to accept him as the executioner of Athaliah. One of the most brilliant moments of the play occurs when the High Priest has a prophetic vision and sees that his own son will be put to death by Joash, when the latter is King. Because Jehoiada accepts the death of his son for the sake of God, we can accept him humanly as Athaliah's executioner.

Athaliah is caught in the temple. The Levites surround her. She sees Joash crowned. Abner deserts her. The Queen knows she is doomed, and dooms herself once again:

> Then let the boy be King . . .
> And may the symbol of God's victory
> Be my own grandson's dagger stuck in me! †

The Queen, about to die, foresees, though, that her grandson will eventually desert David and act as if he were Ahab's heir:

---

* Sainte-Beuve, *Port-Royal.*
　† *Qu'il règne donc ce fils . . .*
　　Et que, pour signaler son empire nouveau,
　　On lui fasse en mon sein enfoncer le couteau!
　　　　　　　　　　　　(Act V, scene 6)

Rebellious to Your wish, indifferent to Your will
This grandson of Ahab shall confound You still!
He'll flee Your law—I see it—even toward Hell!
The avenger of Athaliah, Ahab, and Jezebel! *

Athaliah, who grows weaker throughout the play wooing her own destruction, at the last foresees and boldly asserts the future treachery to the God of her destroyer. Having died so many times in her imagination, when she finally is about to be executed, she prophesies her future vengeance.

With Athaliah's last speech, Racine completed the old Queen's life in tragedy, and his own career as a tragic poet.

---

* *Conforme à son aïeul, à son père semblable,*
On verra de David l'héritier détestable
Abolir tes honneurs, profaner ton autel,
Et venger Athalie, Achab et Jézabel.

(Act V, scene 6)

METATHEATRE

Hamlet *Q.E.D.*

PEOPLE HAVE GROWN TIRED, I suspect, of thinking about *Hamlet;* also, of reading further explanations of the play. Will not each new interpretation prove to be a misinterpretation—the moment, that is, it stops being new? This is what has happened again and again, to theory on theory, explanation after explanation, many of which began by provoking our interest—only to disappoint us as wrong.

Yet if *Hamlet* is to be clearer when read and less embarrassing when produced, we do need an interpretation of it. And it is to be feared we need the right one. . . .

Can anyone be right where so many have been wrong, the most ingenious and the most erudite, the most systematic and profound? Yet the many wrong explanations already advanced have surely reduced the possible chances for error now. Moreover, the main error of past critics can finally be generalized. Not a doubt of it—the best critics of *Hamlet,* like Goethe, Coleridge, and A. C. Bradley, were overly psychological in their approach to the play; concentrating on its content, they ignored the problem of its form. And T. S. Eliot has even justified their error as inevitable, asserting, in a now famous essay, that the content of *Hamlet* is so psychologically complicated its form could not but be obscure. Then how could its form be analyzed? Eliot's view, in fact, marks a turning point in the history of *Hamlet* criticism. If Eliot was right, then a purely literary or dramatic analysis of *Hamlet* would have to be barren; the real explanation of the play's difficulties must be left to psychologists.

Since Eliot's essay, of course, other critics have defended the form of the play; they defended the play as tragedy. In so doing, I think, they have ignored or glossed over *Hamlet*'s very real difficulties. So that of the two views, (1) that *Hamlet* is defective as tragedy and (2) that *Hamlet* is a tragedy and great, the first must be preferred.

But a third view is possible. What if our own misunder-

standing of the form of *Hamlet* has made its content seem
so complicated? What if *Hamlet* is not essentially a tragedy? Then the play might be explained without our having
to psychoanalyze either Shakespeare or Hamlet—as if this
were even possible, when we have no biography of Shakespeare to guide us!

Surely it is at least theoretically possible that Shakespeare
in the process of writing *Hamlet,* finding it difficult to make
the story tragic, and personally inclined to treat it differently, turned toward various play-within-a-play devices,
but did not indicate his purpose clearly, still calling *Hamlet*
a tragedy. My guiding assumption is, to be sure, that it was
quite impossible in the age of Elizabeth for any dramatist,
including Shakespeare, to make a true tragedy of Hamlet's
story.

Could Shakespeare's *Hamlet* have been a tragedy? Now,
my aim is not to add still another question to those already
raised by the play. Answering this question, I hope to answer all the old questions—once and for all.

II

Would *Hamlet* have been a tragedy if the Ghost had told
Hamlet to kill his mother, along with Claudius? Instead of
this, as we know, the Ghost expressly forbids Hamlet to
harm his mother in any way, urging him to "leave her to
heaven," and devote his energies to killing his uncle. But
it is not tragic to kill one's uncle nor to have been told
to do so, even by one's father's ghost. Hamlet, so ready
for tragedy in his attitude and character, with such a perfect disposition for the part, is asked by his father's ghost
to do something of little tragic consequence.

A great deal has been made of the fact that having been
urged to kill Claudius, Hamlet delays. But what if Hamlet
had actually killed the King, his uncle, forthwith? Would
the play then have been a tragedy? What if Gertrude had
committed suicide? Then Hamlet would have killed his
mother, though indirectly, and would have had to sustain
the inevitable remorse. Still, even if done in that way, the
story of Hamlet would have been a weak one, far weaker
than that of Orestes in the *Oresteia* of Aeschylus or of
Orestes and Electra in the *Electra* of Sophocles. More-

over there is very little in Shakespeare's play to indicate
that Gertrude would have committed suicide had Hamlet
killed Claudius. Gertrude, as Shakespeare conceived her, is
not of an age or character to feel so intemperately about
the loss of any particular husband.

Why did the Ghost not tell Hamlet to kill his mother, as
Apollo in the *Oresteia* told Orestes to kill Clytemnestra? It
will be said that in *Hamlet* the role of Gertrude in the murder of Hamlet's father was left ambiguous. But Shakespeare
could have made Gertrude a participant in the murder, had
he wanted to.

III

In his excellent book, *Greek Tragedy*, Professor Kitto
has made a number of points which, had he related them
to *Hamlet*, would have been invaluable for solving the play's
difficulties. Strangely enough, Kitto takes no account of
these insights in the essay on *Hamlet* in his *Form and
Meaning in Drama*. But in his discussion of Greek tragedy,
Kitto compares three plays by the three Greek writers of
tragedy, Aeschylus, Sophocles, and Euripides, the plays
dealing with the murder of Clytemnestra and Aegisthus by
Orestes and Electra. In the play of Aeschylus, Apollo un-
ambiguously orders Orestes to kill his mother. Kitto makes
the point that since the command to kill his mother comes
from a god, Orestes, in Aeschylus' drama, is able to kill
Aegisthus first and then Clytemnestra, without shocking
the Greek audience. But in Sophocles' play about the same
event, it is less sure—Sophocles was less religious than
Aeschylus—that Apollo in fact ordered Orestes to kill his
mother. As a result, according to Kitto, Sophocles did not
dare end the play with the murder of Clytemnestra by her
son, but instead, made Orestes kill Clytemnestra first and
then Aegisthus. This is already a great weakening of the
tragic climax as compared with the version of Aeschylus.

Next, Kitto takes up Euripides' *Electra*. Euripides was,
of course, far more rationalistic than Sophocles; in Euripides' play, Apollo is judged, says Kitto, as ". . . neither
the defender of some principle in society nor the embodi-
ment of a universal law; he was simply the god of Delphi,

an immoral and reactionary institution. Therefore he [Euripides] brings the god out of the enigmatic background in which Sophocles had placed him, makes him command the act of vengeance, and makes that as repulsive as he can." As a result, the killing of Aegisthus and Clytemnestra by Orestes and Electra is a melodramatic event, showing the avengers as despicable and personally motivated; the victims appear somewhat better than their murderers. The murder committed by Clytemnestra and Aegisthus is in the past; the guilty pair have not just murdered Agamemnon when they are killed by Orestes. From the point of view of Euripides, the present murder becomes worse than the past murder; there is no feeling in his play of either necessity or justice. No cosmic piety is suggested in the motivation of either Electra or Orestes. Their motives are without metaphysic, and we respond to their deed with horror.

The comparison of these three Greek plays with *Hamlet* casts a new light on the difficulties faced by Shakespeare when he set out to make a tragedy of a story so similar to the one Aeschylus had treated greatly, the less religious Sophocles handled subtly, and the skeptical Euripides reduced to violent melodrama. It should be noted, too, that whoever the man was, we have a right to infer that the author of Shakespeare's plays was even less religious than Euripides. Some have questioned this judgment and argued that Shakespeare, if not a believing Christian, had at least a "Christian sensibility." Perhaps. But even if we assume Shakespeare to have had some measure of Christian belief, how could such belief have helped him in making a tragedy of Hamlet's story? The Christian God, with the supernatural realms of hell, purgatory, and heaven at his disposal, could scarcely be imagined as intervening in a human action for a this-world vengeance. The God of the Old Testament, like the Greek gods, had, of course, an interest in this-world solutions.

Shakespeare was, moreover, quite without Euripides' very evident taste for melodrama. Most of Shakespeare's tragedies are defective; they are failures at tragedy, not efforts to write melodrama: *Lear, Othello, Coriolanus, Julius Caesar, Timon of Athens* are inadequate tragedies, if we take that form seriously. But we can assume that Shakespeare did not want these plays to be melodramatic, just as we can assume he did not want them to be imperfect.

The act of revenge, to which Hamlet is commanded, could not be justified religiously by Shakespeare. Would his play, then, have to be a melodrama like Euripides' *Electra*?

IV

Let us assume that Shakespeare has resolved to write his *Hamlet* and does not know how to make the story tragic. If the Prince obeys the injunction of the Ghost and kills his uncle, there is no tragedy; if the Prince kills his mother without a divine order, there is no tragedy either; then how could the play be a tragedy at all? With these questions, which Shakespeare may never have put, we come closer to his intention and to his peculiar resolution of the drama he set himself to write. Since there could be no tragedy in prompt action on Hamlet's part, Shakespeare dignifies Hamlet's inactivity, making it philosophic.

So we have the wonderful soliloquy on being and non-being, which quickly becomes a question put by Hamlet as to whether or not he should take his own life. But if it is better to be dead than to live, then how could killing Claudius avenge the murder of Hamlet's father? If there is a question as to whether one should be or not be, then there is surely no answer as to why Hamlet should kill Claudius. The great soliloquy is a complete contradiction of the assignment given Hamlet; it is much more than that; it is a contradiction of any assignment, of any action. But since we are speaking of a character in a play we are also speaking of that character's author. Shakespeare, too, had no reason to make Hamlet act, and a very strong reason for making him philosophize at the moment of the famous soliloquy.

Thus it is that Shakespeare, with his unfailing feeling for the common, appealed to a very gross opinion, that thought and action contradict each other. This opinion has helped make Hamlet loved by audiences, who feel him to be a victim, not of his situation, but of his thought.

V

. The psychoanalytic critics have said that Hamlet could
not kill Claudius because he desired his mother as Claudius
desired her; they also suggest that Hamlet wanted his
father's death, which Claudius encompassed. According to
them, Hamlet could not have avenged his father, since he
wanted what Claudius got. The psychoanalytic view thus
converts Hamlet into a figure of envy; he envies the resolute
action by which a man gets what he wants, no matter what
the means. The two objects of Hamlet's envy are Claudius
and Fortinbras, Claudius because he has killed Hamlet's
father and gotten both Hamlet's mother and Denmark,
Fortinbras because he is leading a military action likely to
be crowned with success. In this view, Hamlet represents
the envy of thought for action, be that action despicable
or heroic. I submit that Hamlet, as Shakespeare has presented him in the play, is totally lacking in envy. Even
when he expresses admiration for whoever "can find quar-
rels in a straw," he seems to us like one who has discovered
a good where he has not suspected it, and not like one who
has a hankering to be somebody else. No, I say, Hamlet's
philosophizing about action is a projection into the play of
the playwright's difficulty in making his hero tragic.

VI

Shakespeare, to dignify Hamlet's inactivity, gave it, as I
have said, a philosophic quality. Those critics who have
considered Hamlet the victim of his own irresolution, be-
guiled by this notion, have lost sight of the dramatic movement of the play as a whole. What is that movement?
When this movement is grasped, the new form Shakespeare
would turn to, later in his career, may be glimpsed.

Everyone has noticed that there is a play within a play,
for Hamlet puts on a show in order to catch, as he says, the
"conscience of the King." What has not been noticed,
though, but becomes evident once one abandons the notion
that the play is a tragedy, or that Shakespeare could make
it one, is that there is hardly a scene in the whole work in
which some character is not trying to dramatize another.

Almost every important character acts at some moment like a playwright, employing a playwright's consciousness of drama to impose a certain posture or attitude on another. Here is Gertrude urging Hamlet to look less melancholy:

> Good Hamlet, cast thy nighted color off,
> And let thine eye look like a friend on Denmark.

The sense of Hamlet's reply is that there is that within him which cannot be dramatized:

> 'Tis not alone my inky cloak, good mother,
> Nor customary suits of solemn black,
> Nor windy suspiration of forc'd breath,
> No, nor the fruitful river in the eye,
> Nor the dejected havior of the visage,
> Together with all forms, moods, shows of grief,
> That can denote me truly. These indeed seem,
> For they are actions that a man might play;
> But I have that within which passeth show,
> These but the trappings and the suits of woe.

The next attempt to dramatize Hamlet and impose on him a particular posture comes from the Ghost, whose revelation is couched in the most theatrical and stagey terms. In fact the Ghost tells Hamlet that he could easily, by revealing the secrets of his prison house, produce an immediate effect upon the Prince:

> I could a tale unfold whose lightest word
> Would harrow up thy soul, freeze thy young blood,
> Make thy two eyes, like stars, start from their spheres,
> Thy knotty and combined locks to part
> And each particular hair to stand on end,
> Like quills upon the fretful porpentine.

This is what the Ghost could do to Hamlet. However, he will not, having been forbidden to tell of his supernatural sufferings. All the same, the Ghost is determined to impose on Hamlet a definite posture. At first, Hamlet seems to accept it:

> Yea, from the table of my memory
> I'll wipe away all trivial fond records,
> All saws of books, all forms, all pressures past,
> That youth and observation copied there,
> And thy commandment all alone shall live
> Within the book and volume of my brain . . .

But immediately afterward Hamlet retaliates against the Ghost by trying to dramatize him in turn, in the wonderful and otherwise inexplicable scene when the Ghost has disappeared under the boards and Hamlet asks the guards and Horatio to swear that they have seen nothing. The remarkable thing about this scene is the fond contempt with which Hamlet addresses the Ghost, who has just sworn him to devote his whole life to revenge. Hamlet calls the Ghost "boy," "truepenny," "old mole," and "worthy pioneer." How are we to understand these contemptuous epithets addressed by Hamlet to the Ghost of his father? I shall not say that I have a final interpretation of this scene, which, by the way, will move any audience, however they understand it. I suggest, though, that the reaction of Hamlet is that of a man with a playwright's consciousness who has just been told to be an actor, and is now determined to make an actor of the very playwright who had cast him for an undesired role. What makes the Ghost a serious playwright is what has happened to him. He has the force of death and hell behind his stage instructions. Hamlet, however, has the force of his—that is, Shakespeare's—dramatic imagination. The scene is one of the most wonderful in all drama. This is not a struggle between two characters, but between two playwrights. And the better playwright, Hamlet—in terms of consciousness—, happens to be the lesser playwright in terms of zeal. Hence his dramatic retaliation has to be humorous.

Is not any son forced to be an actor in his parents' script? They chide him, spank him, dress him, coddle him, order him around: to be a child means to take direction. (Actors in general are childish.) Certainly Hamlet, as a child, must have been through all that. But having been in the play of his parents, almost any individual will want to be in another play, when grown up. Besides, it was not Hamlet's father who authored the situation he asks Hamlet to play a part in. The author of this situation was Hamlet's uncle. Who could want to become an actor in a bloody show put on by a villainous uncle? Certainly not Hamlet.

Polonius, who dramatizes himself as wise, treats his son Laertes and his daughter Ophelia as if they were actors in a play whose meaning he, Polonius, alone understands. In

the famous speech Polonius makes to Laertes, he even tells
the young man the kind of clothes he should wear, the
kind of figure he should cut. With more at stake, Polonius
instructs Ophelia on how to test Hamlet's real intentions
toward herself and toward the King. Ophelia obeys her
father's directions, but Hamlet, with his sensitivity to stage
technique, sees through her guise of innocence at once.
Polonius, who is able to dramatize both his son and his
daughter, does not try to dramatize Hamlet; this is because
Polonius, amateur playwright that he is, thinks Hamlet is
already dramatized, and that he, Polonius, knows exactly
the plot of the drama Hamlet is in: Hamlet is infatuated
with Ophelia, cannot expect to marry her, and hence is
melancholy. Everything Polonius does follows from this
fancy, in which he believes as completely as a bad playwright in his crude plot. Finally Polonius goes too far, spies
on Hamlet's violent scene with his mother, and is killed by
Hamlet, who mistakes him for the King.

Ernest Jones maintains that Hamlet did not mistake
Polonius for the King, and would have been incapable of
killing the latter. The psychoanalytic critic has not taken
into account how useless it would have been to Shakespeare's purpose for Hamlet to kill Claudius at any moment
before the end of the fifth act. The "mystery" of Hamlet's
incapacity has at least as much to do with dramatic form
as with psychology. What is most interesting in the scene,
though, is that two playwrights are present in it, Polonius
behind the arras, and Hamlet, who gives his mother a
playwright's instructions about her future behavior: she
is to avoid her husband's bed, and, as Hamlet indicates,
by making such avoidance habitual, she may be able to
arrive at a truer consciousness of her responsibilities. In
this scene Hamlet urges his mother to act without sincerity
until that moment when her motives, by force of repeated
acting, become sincere. At this point it is necessary for a
third playwright to put in an appearance. The Ghost does
just that, appearing to Hamlet and reminding him that he,
so eloquent in instructing his mother how to act, has forgotten his own role, which is to kill Claudius.

Two vain and very minor playwrights are quickly called
upon by Claudius. These are Rosencrantz and Guildenstern,

who first try to find out what is in Hamlet's mind and are told by him that they cannot play on him. Nor can they. Their final instructions are to dramatize Hamlet as a corpse when he sails with them for England. They have sealed orders requesting his execution on arrival. Hamlet, of course, rewrites the orders, and when the three arrive in England, Rosencrantz and Guildenstern are executed instead of him.

All of the characters in the play can be distinguished as follows: some are fundamentally dramatists* or would-be dramatists, the others are fundamentally actors. Thus Gertrude and Ophelia are actors; so is Laertes; but Hamlet, Claudius, Polonius, and the Ghost are dramatists. There is still another dramatist, whose dramaturgy in the end Hamlet will consent to.

This dramatist is death. When Hamlet has returned from England, after having defeated the crude intrigue of Claudius, Rosencrantz, and Guildenstern, he is ready for death. As he says, "the readiness is all." He passes with Horatio by the cemetery, sees the gravedigger at work, and finds the skull of Yorick, the court clown he had loved. At this moment Hamlet recognizes the truth of that dramatic script in which no one can refuse to act: death will make us all theatrical, no matter what we have done in life. The skull is pure theatre. It is a perfect mask. I think it is at this moment that Hamlet accepts death's dramaturgy, not his father's, not his own. He is ready to die now, no matter what the occasion.

What is the meaning of Hamlet's words to Horatio urging the latter not to die: "Absent thee from felicity awhile"—if not that death's dramaturgy is finally the most felicitous? Hamlet had found the terrible dramatist who

---

* In calling the important characters of *Hamlet* "playwrights," am I relying on a metaphor? To an extent, yes. On the other hand, I claim that no other metaphor could throw an equal light on the play's movement. Suppose that we called Hamlet, the Ghost, Claudius, and Polonius "poets" and compared their rhetoric. This could be done, and might lead to some discovery. But not, I think, to any important discovery about the play as a whole. When I say that the important characters are "playwrights" what I want to underscore is that each of them has the consciousness of a dramatist as well as that of a character.

could dramatize even him. And this is why he falls in with the crude, melodramatic scheming of Claudius; the latter promotes a duel between Hamlet and Laertes. There could be no cruder plotting. The foil of Laertes is poisoned, and there is a poisoned wine for Hamlet to drink if, after exertion, he needs refreshment. Hamlet gives not the slightest thought to the details of the duel, and acts as if he suspects nothing. He is ready now to be in the worst play possible, to act in it, play his part, pretend to believe in it; he has not accepted the role the Ghost has tried to force on him, but the role from which he cannot escape anyway, the role death will inevitably make him play. The miserable melodrama of Claudius proceeds to its climax. Laertes wounds Hamlet, they exchange foils, Hamlet wounds Laertes and the latter tells him that they will both die from the poison on the foils. It is only then that Hamlet kills Claudius. Dying, he does what he could not do when hoping to live.

VII

I have said that there are four playwrights among the characters of *Hamlet*: Claudius, the Ghost, Polonius, and Hamlet. What kinds of playwrights are they; in other words, what kinds of plays are they capable of?

Claudius is a writer of melodrama from start to finish. He kills his brother horribly, pouring into "the porches of his ear a leprous distillment"; the peculiar detail that the poison was poured into the victim's ear and not given him to drink, as would be more natural, suggests the creator of a sensational story, as well as an assassin.

The Ghost is a typically Elizabethan writer of melodrama; though himself tragically victimized, killed by his brother, and subject to eternal punishment in hell, all he requires of Hamlet is the murder of Claudius. He expressly forbids Hamlet to harm Gertrude in any way. His conception of life, even after death, is extremely gross: he wants what began as tragedy to end as melodrama.

Polonius is the amateur playwright par excellence. Though caught in the bloody intrigue of Denmark's royal family, he looks forward to a happy and practical con-

summation of events fraught with terror. He thinks that
his plotting will resolve the problems of Denmark and of
his daughter's relationship with Hamlet. When killed, in
the third act, he has not the faintest notion of what will
happen in the fourth or the fifth. But his daughter dies a
suicide, his son dies a murderer. No playwright could have
been more mistaken in his understanding of events than
Polonius, striving to control all the other characters by
intrigue.

What kind of playwright is Hamlet? This question is
more difficult to answer. Like his creator, he has the most
excellent sense of theatre, as is shown in his advice to the
actors. Certainly Hamlet's melancholy has endowed him
greatly for tragic poetry; but he is in a situation which the
Ghost of his own father has forbidden him to define tragically. Now we can assume Hamlet's taste to be quite
different from the Ghost's. Hamlet, then, with his gifted
playwright's consciousness has the problem of rewriting
the melodrama he has been placed in, but with no alternative form in view. For he has been expressly forbidden to
convert this melodrama into tragedy. Finally, he yields to
the appeal of the one dramatist whose script, like tragedy,
involves necessity and places one beyond chance. This
dramatist is death. In turning toward death Hamlet is turning toward something outside the play, not fated by the
plot as in tragedy, or forced on the plot as in melodrama.
He is considering death and accepting it in its universal
meaning, not as the fate likely to overtake him because of
his particular situation, but as that fate which must overtake anyone, no matter what situation he be in. Death,
which I have called somewhat metaphorically the dramatist
in whose script all must act, Hamlet appeals to as an ultimate form. To a modern consciousness is not death equal
to the immortal gods?

VIII

Let us now see if the questions to which the play has
given rise cannot be settled once and for all. If it is borne
in mind that Hamlet does not know the form of the play
he is in, in other words, that Shakespeare was unable to

make a tragedy of *Hamlet,* the major questions about the play can be answered definitively.

(1) Is Hamlet irresolute? Coleridge and Goethe held this view, though they nuanced their judgments differently. Is Hamlet, on the contrary, resolute? That was A. C. Bradley's contention. These questions become nonsensical when we keep clearly in mind that for a character in a play to be judged either resolute or irresolute, the type or form of play he is in has to be clearly defined. But there is no clear definition for the kind of play Hamlet was placed in by Shakespeare.

(2) Is Hamlet mad? He warns his friends that he may put on an "antic disposition," but we may well wonder whether he does so with any other purpose than to avoid the purposelessness of the plot. No doubt Hamlet enjoys acting as if he were mad. He likes the role no one gave him. In pretended madness there is, of course, a refuge from the seriousness of his task. As a madman, Hamlet can say or do anything he wants to say or do, and at any particular moment. He has been told by his father's Ghost not to express his spontaneous feelings. But pretending to be mad, Hamlet can be himself. Since the structure of the play he is in is so indefinite, and not to his taste, he can only get outside of it by acting as if he were mad.

(3) Is Hamlet in love with Ophelia? He is not. Replying to Laertes' expression of love for Ophelia by her grave, Hamlet does declare:

> . . . Forty thousand brothers
> Could not, with all their quantity of love,
> Make up my sum. . . .

but adds immediately afterward:

> Nay, an thou'lt mouth. I'll rant as well as thou

thus negating his declaration.

Psychoanalysis has established very clearly that no man can love a woman unless he has separated himself from involvement with his own parents. But the psychoanalytic critics obscure the truth of this observation in applying it to Hamlet's feelings for Ophelia. Their claim is that Hamlet *desired* to remain involved with his parents; hence his feelings for Ophelia had to be ambiguous. They forget that it is the plot—a plot Hamlet disliked and did not want to be in—which required him to remain so involved. According to them, the plot corresponds to Hamlet's feeling, and does not contradict it. Here I think they are clearly wrong. Hamlet, in the play he is in, cannot love Ophelia. He would, of course, have preferred to be in another play.

(4) Is Hamlet in love with his mother? There is no evidence for any such assumption, except Hamlet's greater interest in his mother's guilt than in his uncle's, which seems to me perfectly normal.

(5) Does Hamlet believe or not believe in the Ghost? Certainly he believes in the Ghost. The entire action of the play comes from the Ghost's appearing to Hamlet and setting him the most unambiguous of tasks; Hamlet shirks the task, finding excuses for inaction. But the concern and guilt for nondoing which Hamlet expresses throughout imply that he believes in the Ghost's honesty, and ought to obey his command. But what the Ghost has commanded him to do holds no interest for Hamlet.

(6) How is it that the sentinels of Elsinore, as well as Marcellus and Horatio, all see the Ghost, while Gertrude, during the scene in which the Ghost appears to Hamlet in her presence, does not see him? Why should not Gertrude have seen the Ghost too? It has been pointed out that Lady Macbeth does not see the ghost of Banquo, while Macbeth does; but there is no illogic in Shakespeare's one real tragedy: no one but Macbeth sees the ghost of Banquo. There is an illogic in Gertrude's inability to see the Ghost, who is visible to ordinary soldiers. Such illogic would not be possible in a true tragedy.

But this question, raised so many times, suggests a much more interesting one: why did not the Ghost deliberately reveal himself to Gertrude? Why was he not interested in touching *her* conscience? Why was he so exclusively interested in getting Hamlet to kill his murderer? This is in Hamlet's own phrase "a poor ghost." That is to say, one uninterested in tragedy.

(7) When Hamlet in the third act sees Claudius kneeling in prayer and has a chance to kill him, why doesn't he kill him? The explanation Hamlet gives is:

. . . now he is praying;
And now I'll do't—And so he goes to heaven,
And so am I reveng'd. That would be scann'd.

.   .   .

Up, sword, and know thou a more horrid hent.
When he is drunk asleep, or in his rage,
Or in th' incestuous pleasure of his bed,
At gaming, swearing, or about some act
That has no relish of salvation in't,—
Then trip him, that his heels may kick at heaven,
And that his soul may be as damn'd and black
As hell, whereto it goes.

Is this explanation a rationalization by Hamlet of his inability to act? After all, what likelihood is there that Hamlet will have the opportunity to find Claudius physically defenseless at some moment when he is also morally and metaphysically helpless? Certainly Hamlet is expecting too much of chance for us to consider his explanation reasonable. The explanation is illogical in another sense, too. The Ghost has demanded of Hamlet only that he kill Claudius, not that he decide on the supernatural destiny of Claudius' soul. And if Hamlet believed in the reality of a final destiny for the soul, would he not also have had the piety—unless he were willing to incur damnation—to leave that supernatural destiny to the judgment of God? Certainly he was rationalizing his inaction. But I think there is sincerity in what he says. He can find no satisfaction in a mere physical dispatch of his villainous uncle; Hamlet, once again, has little taste for melodrama. What he wants is something more—a deeper, a more ultimate meaning for his act. The only moral significance killing Claudius could have had for Hamlet would have been to kill him in front of Gertrude and thus quicken her conscience.

(8) When Hamlet killed Polonius, did he know Claudius was not behind the arras? The psychoanalytic critics who maintain that Hamlet must have known since he had just left the King praying, have to assume two things:

(a) Hamlet went straight from seeing the King to his mother and did not delay, which he might have done, for all we know. If he did delay, then the King would have had time to get to Gertrude's chamber before Hamlet.

(b) Shakespeare did not know what he was doing in writing the two successive scenes, any more than Hamlet knew what he was doing in either of them. For if Shakespeare had wanted us to think that Hamlet was only pretending to kill the King, knowing all the time the King could not be behind the arras, would Shakespeare have made Hamlet say, looking at Polonius' corpse. "I took you for your better"? Shakespeare certainly knew how to indicate insincerity by speech. He could easily have inflected Hamlet's remark to the dead Polonius in this sense, had he wanted to. The psychoanalytic critics thus have to assume that what Hamlet knew—the King was not behind the arras—was clear to him, the character, and not clear to the author, Shakespeare.

It seems far more plausible to me that what Shakespeare intended in the two successive scenes was to contrast Hamlet's lack of interest in killing Claudius and his very great interest in touching his mother's conscience. Hamlet leaves the King whom he has been sworn to kill and goes to his mother to tell her what she must do. In the first scene, the scene with the King praying, Hamlet is supposed to act and does not. In the second scene, with the queen, he does what we know he likes to do—he directs.

(9) What is the dramatic function of the "To be or not to be" soliloquy? I have remarked already that the soliloquy denies the value of action as such; in speaking as he does, Hamlet takes refuge in philosophy, just as he has already taken refuge in pretended madness. So understood, the soliloquy has only psychological meaning. But I think it also has a function in the play's progress. Hamlet's resort to pretended madness takes him out of the plot; so does philosophizing; but, on the other hand, it is through philosophizing that he finally submits willingly to the crudest plotting of all: Claudius' plot with Laertes to kill him. Hamlet's philosophizing is a meditation on death and not very different from the great speech, "Be absolute for death," in *Measure for Measure,* in which the Duke, disguised as a friar, urges the young and not so serious sinner named, oddly enough, Claudio, to accept death, saying Claudio will thereby find life the sweeter. Hamlet's meditation takes him from the plot into metaphysics, and then, turning him

toward death, enables him to feel something metaphysical in the plot.

IX

We are in a position now to dispose of misconceptions of the play, still widely held. The most important of contemporary interpretations, set forth by Francis Fergusson, has been taken up and restated in a somewhat different form by Professor Kitto. Both claim that the play is about the purification of Denmark, that it is a ritualistic play, in which Hamlet is the tragic protagonist whose duty it is to clean up a moral mess for which he is not personally responsible but in which he is personally involved. The notion here is that the problem of Hamlet is to. cleanse society, the society of Denmark, befouled by his uncle's crime.

Fergusson, of course, has tried to explain *Hamlet* in terms of Sophocles' tragedy, *King Oedipus*. But in Sophocles' play it is stated at the very outset that a plague is afflicting the inhabitants of Thebes. Oedipus understands at once that he must do something to lift the plague, and the oracle has declared that the way to do this is to discover the murderer of Laius. Thus the problem posed at the start in Sophocles' tragedy is one involving the people of Thebes and the gods. Later it will be seen that it involves Oedipus and his family. But at the outset of *Hamlet* there is no problem about the state of Denmark, and there is little indication that the people groan under the rule of Claudius, or suffer from his substitution of himself for Hamlet's father. True, there are some details to indicate that Hamlet is not satisfied with the political and social health of Denmark, but these are not too many, nor are they striking. Oedipus is told first that his city is afflicted, and second that the reason for its affliction is a moral disorder, which he determines to uncover. Hamlet has first the premonition of a moral disorder; then he is told what the disorder is. But—and this is the essential point—there are no important signs of the effect of Claudius' crime upon the kingdom. While there is certainly something rotten in Denmark, yet Denmark is as certainly not rotting. And the

Ghost does not ask Hamlet to save society but to avenge *him*. The Ghost does say:

> Let not the royal bed of Denmark be
> A couch for luxury and damned incest,

but this moral-political statement is obviously secondary, an afterthought. For there is no indication whatsoever that for the royal bed of Denmark to be a couch for luxury and damned incest will have any important effect on the inhabitants of that kingdom. Evil is a problem for Hamlet—not for Denmark.

What I have most against this interpretation of the play is the effort of both Fergusson and Kitto to assimilate it to an older work, when it conspicuously marks a point of division between the Greek world and ours. Kitto and Fergusson interpret the play in the light of Sophocles' *Oedipus*, first, no doubt, because Freud has made the figure of Oedipus so important, but also because they cannot think of *Hamlet* except as a tragedy; and finding it so unlike any classical tragedy, they were perhaps impelled to assimilate it to the most perfect of classical tragedies.

T. S. Eliot judged *Hamlet* a defective tragedy. He was right; as tragedy it is defective. He was wrong, though, in judging the play as tragedy. The interesting point in his essay is his notion that Shakespeare, in writing *Hamlet,* was not able to find the right "objective correlative" for the experience he was trying to express. According to Eliot, Hamlet's feelings are excessive with respect to his situation: he lacks an objective reason for feeling such melancholy and cuts the figure of an adolescent, exaggerating his own anguish and trying to impose on others the norms of an idealism doomed to remain vague.

To be sure, Hamlet is an objective expression of Shakespeare's inability to make of his play a tragedy. But Shakespeare made something else of his play, something quite as extraordinary as tragedy. It is to be noted that Eliot ignores the originality of the character and of the play, too, in which, for the first time in the history of drama, the problem of the protagonist is that he has a playwright's consciousness. Hamlet is not an adolescent; he is the first stage figure with an acute awareness of what it means to be staged. How be dramatized when one has the imagination to be a dramatist? After *Hamlet* it would be difficult for any playwright to make us respect any character lacking dramatic consciousness. In a novel of Unamuno, a character actually rejects the fate chosen for him by the author and demands that the latter change it. The problem of author versus character was I think first envisaged in *Hamlet*. From now on—unless there is to be a new culture whose values we can scarcely foresee—no dramatist has the right to set any supposedly self-conscious character on the stage who does not collaborate in his dramatization. In this sense Jean-Paul Sartre was profoundly correct. No one with self-consciousness can ever do anything drastic in life or on the stage, with our respect, that is, unless he has agreed to his commitment.

What Eliot did not take into account is that none of us, no matter what our situation, really knows the form of the plot he is in, and Hamlet was the first theatrical figure who expressed this fact fully. Doubtless, this is why Hamlet was treated so abusively in Bolshevik criticism; to be sure, the Bolsheviks were interested in criticizing the Hamletism of the Russian intelligentsia. And in this they may have been justified. Turgenev, long before the Bolsheviks appeared, had demanded more Don Quixotes and fewer Hamlets. But I suspect that the Bolsheviks felt a spite against Hamlet that Turgenev could never have known; thinking they knew the real plot of history, the Bolsheviks could not but dislike a theatrical personage who suggests that no one really knows what kind of play he is in. Certainly Hamlet is one of the first characters to be free of his author's contrivances. Some three hundred years later six characters would visit a playwright, who had not invented them, and according to his own testimony, ask him to be their author.

Metatheatre:
Shakespeare and Calderón

I

ONLY CERTAIN PLAYS tell us at once that the happenings
and characters in them are of the playwright's invention,
and that insofar as they were discovered—where there is
invention there also has to be discovery—they were found
by the playwright's imagining rather than by his observing
the world. Such plays have truth in them, not because they
convince us of real occurrences or existing persons, but because they show the reality of the dramatic imagination,
instanced by the playwright's and also by that of his characters. Of such plays, it may indeed be said: "The play's
the thing." Plays of this type, it seems to me, belong to a
special genre and deserve a distinctive name.

But is there not already an adequate name for such plays,
one which has the advantage of being well known? Are
not plays of the kind I mean essentially comedies? We
do not believe that what takes place in comedy has really
occurred: events in comedy are reduced by humor to ex-
amples for reflection and are not irrevocable, as in tragedy.
Nor do characters in comedy have to convince us they exist;
all they have to do is to make us laugh. Humor, I suppose,
consecrates nonexistence. But that which does not exist
can scarcely make us sad. So comedies have to end happily.

It is true that the plays I have in mind end happily in the
main, but many of them are able to do what comedy never
can do, that is, to instill a grave silence—a speculative
sadness—at their close. They can do this without being
tragedies, which means, without making us believe that the
events presented, responsible for our sadness, happened
once and for all. Moreover, such plays make us feel concerned for characters who tell us frankly they were invented to make us feel concerned for them.

Should the plays I am speaking of—if there is any humor
in them—be called tragi-comedies? I object to this self-

contradictory term, which tells us only that humor and
pathos may alternate in a play, but does not define that
kind of play in which humor and pathos may alternate.
Besides, if the events on the stage are not irrevocable,
then wherein lies their tragic content? If the events are irrevocable, wherein lies their comedy? The term tragi-
comedy implies, it seems to me, two different kinds of
plays, amalgamated no one knows just how. If it is said:
by the "genius" of the playwright—is that not asking the
playwright's genius to do the critic's task?

Remember, too, the scorn no less a genius than Shakespeare showed for those satisfied to combine very different
dramatic terms, with no clearer concept for joining them
than that provided by the hyphen. The false sage, Polonius,
whose words, to Hamlet's thinking are "Buzz, Buzz," announces that the actors just arrived at Elsinore are capable
of doing all manner of plays: "pastoral-comical, historical-
pastoral, tragical-historical, tragical-comical-historical-pas-
toral."

Surely the plays I am referring to should not be described
so variously. Some of them can, of course, be classified as
instances of the play-within-a-play, but this term, also well
known, suggests only a device, and not a definite form.
Moreover, I wish to designate a whole range of plays, some
of which do not employ the play-within-a-play, even as a
device. Yet the plays I am pointing at do have a common
character: all of them are theatre pieces about life seen as
already theatricalized. By this I mean that the persons
appearing on the stage in these plays are there not simply
because they were caught by the playwright in dramatic
postures as a camera might catch them, but because they
themselves knew they were dramatic before the playwright
took note of them. What dramatized them originally?
Myth, legend, past literature, they themselves. They represent to the playwright the effect of dramatic imagination
before he has begun to exercise his own; on the other hand,
unlike figures in tragedy, they are aware of their own
theatricality. Now, from a certain modern point of view,
only that life which has acknowledged its inherent theatricality can be made interesting on the stage. From the same
modern view, events, when interesting, will have the quality

of having been thought, rather than of having simply occurred. But then the playwright has the obligation to
acknowledge in the very structure of his play that it was
his imagination which controlled the event from beginning
to end.

Plays of the kind I have in mind exist. I did not invent
them. However, I shall presume to designate them. I call
them metaplays, works of metatheatre.

II

Consider a great seventeenth-century play, Molière's *Tartuffe*. Molière called it a comedy, and it is generally played
as such. Stendhal, however, noticed that he laughed only
twice during a performance of *Tartuffe,* and that the audience around him laughed hardly more. The difficulty in
laughing when *Tartuffe* is performed is not because the
characterization or the plot lacks humor, but because
Tartuffe, the villain, bulks so much larger than his victims,
and is so much more interesting. As French critics have
pointed out, Tartuffe is no hypocrite in the ordinary sense
of pretending to be spiritual in order to satisfy carnal
desires; he is hypocritical in order to be himself: when
he is most hypocritical, then he is most Tartuffe.

Tartuffe happens to be much bigger than the conventional
comedy in which Molière put him. So, if Molière wrote
Tartuffe in order to criticize religious bigotry and moral
hypocrisy, his play is self-defeating: Molière's hypocrite
and bigot is not odious, but interesting to us. No doubt
Molière intended a much different effect. We know from
his other plays how he valued sincerity. Should we think of
Tartuffe, then, as designed to attack something going on in
society, outside the action it presents? But the villain of
that action is not a statement about the world, but a statement about himself. If we refer Tartuffe to the world, he
will give it more meaning, I think, than it could have
without him.* I think, too, he was addressed to the imagination of Molière's audience, while the play he is in

* Tartuffe is a self-referring character: one who has the capacity
to dramatize others, and thus put them in whatever situation he
is intent on being in. He refers to himself because he has the
capacity to make others always refer to him.

was addressed to their social reason. In any case, Tartuffe looms up out of Molière's comedy, greater than it, and destroys it.

But in what kind of play should a character of this imaginative size have been placed? In what kind of play should Hamlet have been put? In *Six Characters in Search of an Author*, perhaps the most original play-within-a-play written in this century, the remark is made that certain dramatic characters—Hamlet is one mentioned—cannot be contained in the works they first appeared in and have had to venture far from their creators into other works by other authors. Now I would say that if Tartuffe and Hamlet seem to break out of the plays and situations they were first placed in, this is not merely because the right dramatic form had not been found for them, but perhaps more importantly, because these characters are themselves dramatists, capable of making other situations dramatic besides the ones they originally appeared in.

Any play written at a certain depth should have some other aim than to suggest social change or moral reform. The contemplative imagination can and does delight in what moral and practical wisdom urges us to reject. We are all more profound than our purposes seem to indicate. And the playwright who ventures to touch us very deeply ought to know that he is touching a part of us which is irrelevant to the achievement of our most rational goals. Molière was, I think, too profound for the form he relied on in *Tartuffe*.

Take another play, an Elizabethan play—a great play, too, but one in which the events are made unreal by the playwright's inability to decide whether they actually happened or not. When he wrote *Doctor Faustus*, Marlowe lacked, I think, a definite dramatic horizon. What kind of play is *Doctor Faustus*? Marlowe thought he had written a tragedy, as Molière thought he had written a comedy in *Tartuffe*. But is Marlowe's Doctor Faustus truly tragic? Do we feel that Faustus actually sold his soul to the Devil, signed his transaction with Hell in his own blood, and thus was enabled to regain youthfulness, pride, power, and lust at the price of eternal damnation? Do we believe when we watch *Doctor Faustus* that anything of this sort ever happened in the same way we believe when we watch *Macbeth* that Macbeth really talked to the witches, murdered Duncan and Banquo, conversed with Banquo's ghost, massacred Macduff's family, and was finally killed by Macduff?

I am convinced that no one genuinely believes the events in *Doctor Faustus* in any such way. Nor are the events adequately understood by Marlowe. For instance, Marlowe should have made it clear that the transaction between Faustus and the Devil was essentially a theatrical one. Faustus, an old man, is asking the Devil to dramatize him as a youth; here we are on the verge of a new theatrical form. But Marlowe thought of the transaction as one in which Faustus became the tragic protagonist in a play written by the Devil. Therefore Faustus had to be damned. But when we think about the story with a little more sophistication, does it not appear that the Devil was the actor and Faust the dramatist, since it was he, Faust, who called upon the Devil to dramatize him? Such was the interpretation Goethe made when he took up the story, and he was able to give it such clarity and lightness—not simply because he was more philosophical than Marlowe, but because the form for a play like his *Faust* had already been invented. Goethe found that form in Shakespeare and in Calderón.*

III

Why is it that neither Marlowe nor Molière was able to invent the dramatic form both needed, Molière for a proper

---

* Goethe saves Faust, perhaps, by applying the logic of appearance. Faust looks serious, well intentioned, and seems to have dignity. I will not go so far as to say that he is saved because he is better looking than Mephistopheles (any actor playing the part, of course, should be), but I will assert that he is saved because he looks better dramatically than the Devil. Mephistopheles, who exhibits so many likable qualities, lacks dignity. In Goethe's play he never convinces us by his appearance that he is entitled to possess Faust's soul. Of the two, it is clear that Faust is the true dramatist, Mephistopheles, yearning to dramatize, a true actor.

presentation of his character Tartuffe,* Marlowe for phantasizing adequately the dealings of Doctor Faustus with the Devil? But then how is it that neither Lope de Vega, Calderón's predecessor, nor Corneille, with whom the great period of French theatre began, nor any of the English dramatists before Shakespeare had been able to lift the play-within-a-play—which many of them used as a device—to a truly philosophic height?

Of all the European dramatists, Shakespeare was the only one possessed by a complete confidence in the power of imagination, not simply in its power to make speech splendid—Marlowe had that, too—but in its power to arrange, order, and judge all manners of persons and every single type of action; in other words, to put the whole world on stage. Generalizing that power of imagination which guided his best inventions, Shakespeare could make his philosopher, Jaques, say, "the world's a stage."

Calderón achieved his great invention not solely from his trust in the imagination but through the influence of two predecessors who anticipated the theatrical form he perfected in *Life Is a Dream*. These were Cervantes and Tirso de Molina.

Cervantes was of course a playwright for a period and has some excellent works to his credit, including a fine tragedy, *Numantia*. But he had little success on the stage and could not compete with the extraordinarily prolific and inventive master of the period, Lope de Vega, whom Cervantes called a monstrosity of nature, meaning by this that

* I do not mean to imply that Molière was lacking in invention. He lifted comedy to a level of artistry and refinement it had never had before nor has had since. Was he perhaps a "victim of his own invention," to use the phrase Nicola Chiaromonte employed about Pirandello? In any case, *The Misanthrope*, which most critics agree is Molière's masterpiece, has difficulties similar to those presented by *Tartuffe*. If you laugh at Alceste, you have to think he is wrong, and then the play is a comedy; but since you tend to think Alceste is right, you do not want to laugh at him, and then what kind of play is it? Ramon Fernandez, in his fine book on Molière, says that in this work Molière subjected his own chosen art of comedy to a certain skepticism. Is there something immoral about a play that is funny? And is this thought in *The Misanthrope*? If so, is not the play close to theatre about theatre? I must confess I cannot answer this last question to my own satisfaction.

Lope de Vega was able to write splendid works without ever pausing to reflect. Reflection was something natural to Cervantes. *Don Quixote* was published just one year after the production of *Hamlet,* and the two works, equally admired, have always been associated by critics. Turgenev said that a true intellectual has to be a Hamlet or a Don Quixote; Melville said these are the only two real characters in literature.

In any case, Don Quixote, though he appears in a novel —the novel of an ex-playwright—projects in the most complete and perfect way the dramatic horizon of all plays about self-referring characters. Don Quixote is, of course, his own dramatist, and, if we can use modern terms, his own director, his own set man, his own stage manager. He seeks out those situations he wants to play a part in; he will not wait for life to provide them in a natural way. He calls upon his imagination to substitute itself for reality wherever the real is lacking in quality, bravura, excitement, delicacy. His imagination obliges; most often, as in the case of the windmills, to his discomfiture. But Don Quixote is not discouraged. In fact he even learns—for Cervantes' work is in some ways a *Bildungsroman*—how to develop and refine his own taste for illusion. He grows wiser before our eyes in his lust for great adventure.

Then, of course, Calderón had seen the Don Juan of Tirso de Molina (from which Molière took his own masterpiece). Tirso's play was no comedy, but it was certainly not a tragedy. Molina had invented not only a new theatrical type in the figure of Don Juan, but also a new kind of event which certainly does not convince us by its plausibility. The event in fact is utterly implausible, but one of the greatest imaginative creations in dramatic art. The statue of the dead commander—Don Juan had killed the commander in a duel—invites Don Juan to dinner, dines with him, and then carries him off to hell. It is hard to think of any event less believable—or which affects us more powerfully.

Calderón, who had been trained as a theologian, was more logical than Shakespeare and had behind him the great creations of Cervantes and Tirso de Molina. He had himself experimented with almost every known dramatic form: cloak and dagger plays, romantic comedy, tragedy, and farce. Finally, he wrote a number of plays addressed purely to the metaphysical imagination. These are *Devotion to the Cross, The Great Magician,* and perhaps the most perfect play-within-a-play, *Life Is a Dream.* So profound is the appeal of these plays by Calderón, addressed to the metaphysical imagination mainly, that they cannot fail to touch the imagination on every level. Shakespeare, on the other hand, in writing *The Tempest,* was appealing to every level of the imagination, thus including the metaphysical.

IV

Shakespeare experimented throughout his whole career with the play-within-a-play, sometimes introducing play-within-a-play sequences in his tragedies, almost always introducing such sequences in his comedies. *As You Like It, A Midsummer Night's Dream, Twelfth Night, All's Well That Ends Well* are not really comedies, for we cannot account for the pleasure we take in them in terms of their humor, which is often labored, sometimes gross. These are all works of the imagination; but saying this does not define their character or indicate the perfection of form they prefigure. Again, in his chronicles, Shakespeare introduced play-within-a-play sequences, notably in *Henry IV;* by doing so, he was able to set on the stage one of his greatest characters, Falstaff. Falstaff is nothing if not a dramatist,* for not only is he witty himself, but he is the cause of wit in others. Acting, he causes those near him to act in their turn and sets the stage for his own superlative performances.

---

* Falstaff is a self-referring character par excellence, being a dramatist. A witty eighteenth-century writer, Morgann, was led to speculate on Falstaff's birth, parentage, childhood, early associates, and adventures *before* Falstaff's appearance in Shakespeare's play. True, Morgann's essay on Falstaff, defending his character, led to a new, misleading kind of criticism. On the other hand, one cannot think Morgann completely wrong in his observations and judgments. It was objected that Morgann's mistake was to take Falstaff for a real person, instead of as a character in a play. But this character, being essentially a dramatist, can be said to have the capacity and impulse to exist apart from the playwright who created him. Falstaff, the creation of Shakespeare, is himself a creator. Morgann must have felt this.

Dramatizing not only his cronies but even his Prince, Falstaff elicits in them the desire to dramatize him. Our pleasure in those episodes of *Henry IV* involving Falstaff springs from his spontaneous dramaturgy. He makes the tavern wonderful as he makes the battlefield livable—for him.

At the heart of the play there is a question—who will plot the career of Prince Hal? Will it be Prince Hal's father, Henry IV, or will it be Jack Falstaff? If Jack Falstaff, then Prince Hal is almost certain to be defeated or eclipsed by Hotspur. But if Henry IV, less interesting than Falstaff, is able to plot his son's career, then the young man has at least a chance of becoming Henry V. Great issues are at stake here, between the lively, fat knight and the dying King.

We should not understand merely as comedy the fantastic scene in the tavern when Falstaff, acting the part of Henry IV, urges Prince Hal to do the very contrary of what his father desires: "Peremptorily," says Falstaff, playing the King, "I speak it, there is virtue in that Falstaff. Him keep with, the rest banish." Prince Hal and Falstaff then change roles, the Prince playing Henry IV and stating his father's objections to the knight; the latter this time defending himself: "But for sweet Jack Falstaff, kind Jack Falstaff, true Jack Falstaff, valiant Jack Falstaff, and therefore more valiant, being, as he is, old Jack Falstaff, banish not him thy Harry's company, banish not him thy Harry's company. Banish plump Jack, and you banish all the world!" But when Prince Hal is crowned Henry V, he does banish Falstaff, and in words hot with hate.

The scenes involving Falstaff and Prince Hal are pure theatre, of the most imaginative kind. But they are set, after all, in a historical play, where the actual fortunes of the King and the Prince must be dominant. Falstaff is too large for a purely historical drama; he is greater and more interesting than Henry IV, greater and more interesting than Prince Hal. And so we are dissatisfied by Henry V's harshness to him. We cannot help but feel that the king of the tavern was greater than the King of England. This is not the right feeling to have in a work celebrating one of the better rulers of Britain.

Thus *Henry V*, in which Falstaff does not appear at all

—we merely hear of his death—is more unified and play-able than *Henry IV*, which Falstaff dominates imaginatively, but cannot dominate in fact. The play cannot contain him.

The feeling that characters can be superior to their situa-tions may have suggested to Shakespeare the idea for his treatment of Hamlet. Why not for once justify the great character stuck with a bad plot? I think Shakespeare did just that in *Hamlet,* and created his most popular figure—for who, unhappy, will not be consoled by thinking that the plot he is in is at fault, and his soul greater than his fate? "Nature," says Hamlet, "cannot choose its origins." He, Hamlet, could not choose his own mother. This is what dis-turbs him, not lust for her, as the psychoanalytic critics have insisted.*

Yet Shakespeare must have desired to produce a work of a formal structure not incompatible with the presence in it of a greatly conceived character. He achieved this in one tragedy: *Macbeth.* That kind of absolute success he never achieved with the play-within-the-play until he wrote *The Tempest. Measure for Measure* is wonderfully structured, a new kind of philosophical drama; but there is no great character in it. *Cymbeline* and *A Winter's Tale* are fascinat-ing works, but finally must be judged as exercises which made *The Tempest* possible. In *The Tempest,* Shakespeare presented two of his greatest figures, and in a work as great as they are.

The Tempest tells not of a utopia, but of a utopian event, a perfect revolution, which restores the true ruler of Milan, after he has been deposed by the treachery of his brother. Events in life are generally so imperfect that to think of a revolution accomplished without bloodshed and to music seems like dreaming. Some dreams are antithetical to thought; the particular dream actualized in *The Tempest* is not. For a perfect revolution is not theoretically impossible. Such a revolution, of course, has never occurred.

The hero of *The Tempest* is the deposed duke, Prospero. He has acquired a power not precisely political: magic. His

* Hamlet is possessed of a dramatist's imagination to the high-est degree. And, of course, he has appeared again and again in literature and drama, bearing his own name or a pseudonym like Stavrogin or Lorenzaccio.

power is, I think, the magic of thought. This power he uses like a dramatist, creating a false tempest which causes the shipwreck (on the island Prospero rules) of his brother and of his brother's chief supporters. Thrown on Prospero's island, the false Duke of Milan, his counselors, and his son Ferdinand become actors who have lost their cues and do not know how to perform. Ignorant of where they are and misunderstanding their roles, they are easily dominated by Prospero.

Prospero has two servants: the spirit Ariel, who carries out his imaginative orders, and the very body of all bodies, Caliban, who performs certain physical labors, albeit unwillingly. Never was a playwright better served: his theatre an island, his villain the brother who has wronged him and is now at his mercy, his choreographer a spirit, his stagehand the monstrous Caliban.

(I must interpolate here that neither Ariel nor Caliban is properly represented in productions of the play. Ariel should not be seen at all, being too delicate for visual representation. Caliban, on the other hand, is too gross for us to look at. There is something sublime about his grossness; and what is sublime, as Kant noted, lacks form. We should never see more than some part of Caliban's body—a tremendous foot, a huge hand, perhaps for one moment a masklike head covering the whole stage. His voice should not be unlike the tempest which caused the shipwreck of the treacherous Duke. Certainly Caliban should never be represented naturalistically, and the attempt to do just that has spoiled productions of *The Tempest* to this date. I must add that Caliban is in the purest sense a self-referring character, that is to say, a dramatist. One does not need the play to understand him, although unlike Hamlet and Falstaff he is at home in the play he was put in. But a character of this sort can visit other minds, as Caliban did when he visited the mind of Browning, who was then able to write "Caliban upon Setebos," in which Caliban is seen dramatizing the universe and even its creator.)

What of Prospero himself? Some have said that he is none other than Shakespeare, and that Prospero, drowning his book and breaking his staff, is Shakespeare deciding to quit the stage and retire as a country gentleman. I shall not venture to correlate Prospero's action with any so-called fact of Shakespeare's life. But some correlation between Shakespeare and Prospero is justified.

Certainly the events of *The Tempest* were put on by a dramatist. Prospero controls these events throughout, and at the end, attains what he desires through his art. It is then that he gives up his art.

It must be admitted that there is something unpleasant about Prospero: he lacks the naïveté to appear in any drama not produced by him. Shakespeare makes this quite clear. When at ease, in a form congenial to him, Shakespeare was capable of judging with utter impartiality. (Thus he is able to judge jealousy and infidelity without prejudice in a non-realistic work like *A Winter's Tale,* as he is unable to do in *Othello,* which he conceived as tragedy.)

Prospero has the values and disvalues of consciousness to the highest degree. Such a man will strive never to be the actor in someone else's play. Will he try to make others actors in his own story? The temptation is there for anyone with that much power of thought. Perhaps this is why, finally, Prospero breaks his staff and drowns his book "deeper than any plummet ever sounded." His final act implies acceptance of the role life gave him originally, and which he did not invent, and which he will no longer be able to control by thought. Prospero will perhaps not be so unpleasant when he no longer is in charge of events.

But having ventured to use theatrical means to their magical limit, Prospero understands that in some sense all of life is a pageant or show, and he carries this thought to its ultimate consequence, foreseeing that the earth, "the great globe itself," will dissolve, leaving not a rack behind.

Wonder, including metaphysical wonder, is, in *The Tempest,* part of the motivation of the principal figures Caliban, Ariel, and Prospero. Wonder, even metaphysical wonder, has set the stage with the simple direction for the first scene: "a ship at sea." It is expressed in the personality of Prospero's daughter, Miranda, when she first sees Ferdinand, and in Ferdinand himself when he dreams not only of his own father's death but of his father's father's death before him. We wonder at Caliban, Ariel, and Prospero. We watch every character in the play being forced to won-

der. The play, in its characters, story, setting—except for
some jarring moments of low comedy—is all of a piece.

There is a thesis by a German writer attempting to prove
that Calderón must have read *The Tempest* and, influenced
by Shakespeare's play, wrote *Life Is a Dream*. As I have
already indicated, it is not necessary to account for Calderón's great play by any such hypothesis. If we look for influ-
ences on Calderón, they exist in the Spanish theatre and literature. Calderón did not have to read Shakespeare to think
the world a stage or that life can best be represented when
felt to be a dream. All this the Spanish playwright could
glean from Cervantes' great novel.

There is still further reason for not associating *Life Is a
Dream* with any work by Shakespeare. The latter, as I have
tried to show, felt the need to rationalize and purify the
play-within-a-play form in order to accommodate to it characters of a certain imaginative size who would not be at
home in tragedy or comedy, in chronicle or farce. Calderón
needed the theatrical form he perfected in *Life Is a Dream*
for quite a different purpose. Calderón had never been a
great creator of character; he could never have felt that a
personage he set in a play was independent of that play.
Yet even in his less significant theatre pieces he always aims
to give the dramatic event the maximum meaning it can
have, to give dramatic action the quality of thought. In
The Great Magician, not a successful play, the event is what
is interesting, not the characters. It seems to me that the
model or paradigm for Calderón of a real event was a true
thought.

Life Is a Dream is a play-within-a-play, and of the most
subtle design. The Prince of Poland, Sigismund, has been
imprisoned by his own father since birth. He has been educated in all those matters which a prince should know, but
he has been kept chained in a cave until his twenty-first
birthday. The reason he has been so treated by his father,
King Basilio, is that just before the Prince was born, the
King, an astrologer, had read in the stars that the child
about to be born would kill both his mother and father. In
partial confirmation of this prediction, Sigismund's mother
had died in giving birth to him. Basilio at once sentenced
the infant to imprisonment. On his twenty-first birthday,

still chained in a cave, Sigismund cries out: "What crime did I commit except that I was born?"

Basilio's drastic treatment of his son is an attempt to prevent the predicted tragedy in which he, Basilio, has been cast as victim. To prevent the play which he has been told is going to terminate with his death, Basilio determines to take responsibility for the drama's conclusion, rewriting it. His play is to be an antitragedy.

On his twenty-first birthday, Sigismund is given a drug, and when he returns to consciousness finds himself in his father's palace and is told that he had merely dreamed he had been in chains. The young Prince, suddenly freed, at once expresses the violence stored up in him. He threatens everyone, hurls a courtier who contradicts him out a window, and menaces the King, his father. The Prince is overpowered, again drugged, and when he recovers consciousness, is told that he had only dreamed he was a prince, that in fact he had never left the cave, never been freed of his chains. As a result of this second extraordinary revelation, which he cannot refute by any facts he knows to be true, Sigismund concludes that all life is a dream, in which our dreaming is of dreams.

But the people have seen the Prince; they know he lives, there is a revolution, and Sigismund is released. He now has his father Basilio at his mercy. Will the prophecy of the stars prove correct? Will the Prince kill his own father? But the Prince spares his father's life, for he has learned that life is a dream. Only virtue is real. (At one point in the play the Prince has dreamed of doing a good action and is told that goodness, even dreamed, is praiseworthy.)

What has happened in this play? A tragedy was predicted, but did not occur. And if it did not, this was because of the dramatic invention of King Basilio, who substituted for the play intended by fate one of his own invention. The tragedy fails. Basilio's play succeeds. Metatheatre has replaced tragedy.

A *Note on Schiller's* Mary Stuart

GOETHE'S CONTEMPORARY, friend, and rival as a playwright, Johann Friedrich von Schiller, had no disaffection toward tragedy and no disinclination for trying his hand at that form. Schiller was more professional in his approach to the stage than Goethe and had greater stagecraft. Yet he never did write a real tragedy. However, his play *Mary Stuart,* which he called a tragedy, is almost convincing as one.

For most of the play we are in the atmosphere of a Shakespearean or Elizabethan tragedy, or attempt at tragedy. The antagonists are royal kinswomen: Elizabeth and Mary Stuart. Mary is Elizabeth's prisoner and Elizabeth can either pardon or execute her rival. Elizabeth, urged by Lord Burleigh, decides, after a violent scene with Mary, for the crueler and politically more prudent action. Until this point in the play the development is more or less conventional and exactly what one would expect in the imitation of an old tragedy. But Schiller introduces something new into the play, which makes it original and which shows that, despite his desire to write a tragedy, he was aware of the age and what it required of consciousness. Elizabeth signs the warrant for Mary's execution. She does not, however, give it to her Secretary of State, Davison, but leaves it for him with an ambiguous order to see it carried out. Davison hesitates. But there is the document signed by Elizabeth. He surrenders it to Lord Burleigh, who wants Mary dead. The execution follows immediately. Elizabeth, when informed of the event, claims she had never ordered it, that she did not mean the warrant to be given to Lord Burleigh. She attacks Davison as if he were responsible for Mary Stuart's death. Davison tries to defend himself, but cannot meet the Queen's anger, which is both real and pretended.

But to make a tragedy of *Mary Stuart,* Schiller would have had to accept Elizabeth, the executioner of Mary, as a noble figure in ordering that execution. I do not think Schiller was motivated in structuring his play by history, as

the play is not strictly true to historical fact. What we have
at the close of *Mary Stuart* is a denial of responsibility for
Mary's death by Elizabeth, who, for the play to be a tragedy,
would have to accept this responsibility.

Schiller presents us with an Elizabeth who wants to pass
off the responsibility for the terrible act to an inferior and
subaltern character. Now in presenting Elizabeth in this
way, Schiller was not, I believe, psychologically unfaithful
to the Elizabeth we know from history. But I think he was
motivated by something deeper than his knowledge of the
record, which he was perfectly willing to tamper with for
dramatic reasons. What he has shown in the play and what
touches us deeply, is the unwillingness of a person noble
enough to destroy another tragically to take responsibility
for such an act. I suspect that inwardly Schiller had no more
belief in tragedy than Elizabeth could have believed she
had the right to execute Mary Stuart. . . .

The Myth of Metatheatre

I HAVE IMAGINED that Aeschylus, leaving the theatre after
a performance of his *Oresteia,* is kidnaped and taken to a
chi-chi Athenian home. He is treated with courtesy, forbidden to leave, and then introduced to his kidnaper, a
young Athenian named Orestes.

"Why have you brought me here?" the Greek playwright
asks. Orestes replies, "I am your greatest admirer, Aeschylus." The dramatist: "Is that supposed to excuse your treatment of me? Release me at once." "No, Aeschylus, you'll
have to stay," responds Orestes. "Besides, I grant you, I
would have no right to do what I did if I had no other feeling for you than admiration. So I must now tell you frankly
that though I admire you greatly, I am critical of you, too,
very critical. Your *Oresteia* begins wonderfully, gets better
as it goes on, rises to the very greatest height of drama, and
then ends miserably. I brought you here to get you to
change the ending of your trilogy. Perhaps you will when

I explain how important this is to me. You took note of my name, didn't you? Whatever concerns Orestes must concern Aeschylus as much."

At this point Aeschylus becomes interested. He has never before heard this criticism of his great work. "I love the end of my play," says Aeschylus. "And if I am to listen to any criticism of it, I must have a glass of wine." He makes himself comfortable and accepts a glass of wine from his host, who then tells him the following story:

"I happen to have the same name as the hero of your play. But my mother was not named Clytemnestra nor my father Agamemnon. Nor was my mother's lover's name Aegisthus. But what Clytemnestra and Aegisthus did to Agamemnon, my mother and her lover did to my father, who fought, Aeschylus, with you at Marathon, and who, like you, killed many a longhaired Mede. When my father returned, my mother and her lover chopped him to death with an ax. I felt that it was my duty, in turn, to do something terrible to them. I did not. No oracle urged me to. Besides, if an oracle had, I would not have believed it. Being enlightened, I was opposed to oracles. Instead of killing the murderers of my father, I became their friend. I looked kindly on my mother's guilty partner in lechery and murder. He likes me, too, and always wants to go to the theatre with me. We both love the theatre. What else is there in life? But most of all I love your play, which is about me, not as I am, but as I should have been. For the truth is I should have killed my mother and her lover, and since I have not done so, my life has become an empty dream. A dream in which the only bit of reality is your play, which I see as often as I can. Now perhaps you can understand why I am so critical as well as so admiring of it. I, Orestes, go to your *Oresteia*. The beginning, as I told you, is wonderful. I see my father murdered, I watch my mother affirming her guilt; then I appear in the second part of the trilogy, and naturally I like that part of the play best. I have been told unequivocally by Apollo himself to kill my mother and her lover. I am going to do so, no matter what my suffering afterward will be, though I do not myself realize to the full how dreadful it will actually be. I kill the murderer, then the murderess. The Furies appear and follow me offstage. I am the object of their divine sadism, which means that my own masochism becomes divine. Then comes the final part of your trilogy. It is made clear that I have undergone much suffering from the vengeful Furies. I take refuge in the Temple of Athene. Apollo and the Furies appear, he for me, they against me. The gods sit in judgment. Their verdict finally is that I am no longer to be punished for killing my own mother! A vulgar arrangement is made between Athene and the Furies; it is a political deal: the Furies are to get some recognition in the State and, in return, are to be less implacable. As for myself, I am cleared of all further guilt, declared free henceforth to do as I please. But, Aeschylus, having killed my mother, what could there be for me to do?

"Aeschylus, you must change the ending of your play. Since I did not kill my mother and can do so now only in imagination, since my real life now consists only in your work, you must make the end of your play as terrible as the beginning. I want to see myself die by torture. Do this for me, and you will have given meaning and worth, on certain occasions—when the *Oresteia* is shown—to an otherwise empty life."

Genet and Metatheatre

I

JEAN GENET'S extraordinary play, *The Balcony*, is most certainly *not* a piece of avant-garde theatre; it is not eccentric or odd; modern, to be sure, it makes no claim to being especially modernistic. The play is neither peculiar nor perverse; yes, *The Balcony* is a new play, but it is not unlike some rather old ones; it is original, but it belongs in a tradition, and that tradition is none other than the great tradition of Western dramaturgy. *The Balcony* is a metaplay; and the metaplay has occupied the dramatic imagination of the West to the same degree that the Greek dramatic imagination was occupied with tragedy.

As I have already said: Shakespeare and Calderón did not write tragedies; at least, they did not write good tragedies. (Shakespeare wrote one great one, *Macbeth;* Calderón, not even one.) What these playwrights did create was a new type of drama, one with very different assumptions from those of Greek tragedy, and with very different effects. Often they produced this characteristic and new form while intent on writing tragedy.

I have asked myself: can I be the first one to think of designating a form which has been in existence for so long a time, about three hundred years? It is a strange and not undramatic fact of life that something shiningly individual will continue to be seen darkly until it has been given a name.

Let us see why tragedy was not the characteristic form of the Elizabethan or Spanish theatre. Why have most Western dramatists, bent on writing tragedy, been unable to do so successfully? Much of their difficulty can be summed up in a single word: self-consciousness. First, the self-consciousness of the dramatist himself, and then that of his protagonists. For consider: if Antigone were self-conscious enough to suspect her own motives in burying her brother Polynices, would her story be a tragic one? Now the Western playwright is unable to believe in the reality of a character who is lacking in self-consciousness. Lack of self-consciousness is as characteristic of Antigone, Oedipus, and Orestes, as self-consciousness is characteristic of Hamlet, that towering figure of Western metatheatre.

Another, insurmountable difficulty: one cannot create tragedy without accepting some implacable values as true. Now the Western imagination has, on the whole, been liberal and skeptical; it has tended to regard *all* implacable values as false.

Let us look for a moment at a typical Western drama which was meant to be a tragedy, seems to be a tragedy, and has, in fact, been so designated. I am referring to Melville's *Billy Budd*. Now in this short novel—it was made into a play by an adapter, and with all its defects, is still the best dramatic work by an American—the young sailor, Budd, accused of mutinous action, but whom the drum court of officers wants to exonerate, is finally sentenced and executed on the insistence of Captain Vere; this is a man whom we have been led to believe appreciates Budd, loves him, and is more convinced of his innocence than any of the other officers. Did Melville then accept as true at least one implacable value: ship discipline on a man-of-war? I do not think so. For why is Melville unable to make Captain Vere's action in demanding Budd's conviction convincing to us, at least to me? I never believed, in reading *Billy Budd*, that it was necessary for the sailor to hang for discipline on the *Indomitable* to be preserved. Moreover, the consciousness of Captain Vere is not expressed in his action, which is simply a mirror reflecting the regulations of the Mutiny Act. Melville was only able to get to the externally tragic ending of his story by depriving Captain Vere, at a crucial moment, of the very kind of self-consciousness he has throughout his work led us to believe Captain Vere possessed. Now for a character not to have self-consciousness is one thing; for a character to be deprived of self-consciousness by the author in order to be capable of representing some implacable value is quite another. Melville, if Captain of the *Indomitable,* would *not* have sentenced Billy Budd to hang. Of course, one can only speculate, but I think Sophocles would have buried his brother in defiance of the State. The Greek playwright's heroine is of the same culture as her creator. So, of course, is Creon, but Captain Vere, at the moment of his dramatic decision, belongs to a world not Melville's. This is one of the superiorities of *Antigone* (it has others) over *Billy Budd*.

But to come back to the metaplay. It is the necessary form for dramatizing characters who, having full self-consciousness, cannot but participate in their own dramatization. Hence the famous lines of Jaques, Shakespeare's philosopher of metatheatre, "All the world's a stage, and all the men and women merely players." The same notion is expressed by Calderón, who entitled one of his works *The Great Stage of the World.* For both the Spanish and the English poet there could not but be an essential illusoriness in reality. We cannot have it both ways: a gain for consciousness means a loss for the reality of its objects, certainly for the reality of its main object, namely the world. Obviously it takes a high degree of consciousness to become aware that the world cannot be proved to exist. However, I shall not insist on this point, for I think the objectivity of the world is maintained not by logic, but, like some fabled treasure which dragons guard, by those monsters to the sensitive and skeptical mind: implacable values. Thus it is that if, in Greek tragedy, the hero is defeated, on the other hand the reality of the world is underscored; in the metaplay, the hero, however unfortunate, can never be decisively defeated, perhaps he can never even be heroic (as Kleist's wonderful *Prince of Homburg* suggests); but on the other hand, the reality of the world is mortally affected, illusion becomes inseparable from reality. *Life Is a Dream* is the title of Calderón's greatest play, and Shakespeare's theatre terminates with the famous: "We are such stuff as dreams are made on." The point I am making here is that these phrases are not chance expressions by Calderón and Shakespeare, but fundamental concepts of the dramatic form which they initiated.

In the metaplay there will always be a fantastic element. For in this kind of play fantasy is essential, it is what one finds at the heart of reality. In fact, one could say that the metaplay is to ordinary fantasy as tragedy is to melodrama. As in tragedy the misfortunes of the hero must be necessary and not accidental, so in the metaplay life *must* be a dream and the *world* must be a stage.

All this would have by now been much clearer if it had not been for the appearance in the nineteenth century of a very great dramatist, Henrik Isben, who tried to give to the realistic play a necessitarian structure like that found in Greek tragedy, and this without sharing the premises of either Sophocles or Aeschylus, Ibsen's own view of the world being actually closer to Shakespeare's and Calderón's. As a result, a wrong belief was propagated—it dominated the stage for more than fifty years—that without the Greek metaphysic the form of tragedy was possible and valid. Now if this view was never formally challenged, its inadequacy was felt by the best playwrights of the present century. Their plays, in the main, are metaplays. Among them is Jean Genet.

The Balcony is a brothel whose clients arrive equipped, in Madame Irma's phrase, "each with his own scenario." Surely this identifies the drama as a metaplay. Among the clients are three more or less nondescript persons, one of whom wants to dramatize himself as a bishop, one as a judge, one as a general. The prostitutes assigned to these men play up their illusions of greatness, degrading them in certain instances, just to make the act seem more real. The Grand Balcony is, indeed, "a palace of illusions." For the clients are fitted out with costumes appropriate to their dreams. We watch them don these costumes as they prepare for peculiar satisfactions. It is to be noted that in watching them change before our eyes from their uncostumed reality to the bravura figures they become when arrayed to act, we get an altogether new feeling of the reality—not of character but of costume. Seldom does it happen in any play, modern or classical, that costume means much to the audience. In most revivals of Elizabethan dramas, costume is actually an impediment to our acceptance of the situation or the scene. Hence directors have experimented with doing the old plays in modern dress. But there is something poetical in costume as such, and the theatre would be disadvantaged by a complete loss of it. In *The Balcony*, Genet has done nothing less than restore the poetical value of costume to the stage. For the fact is that when we see costumes being put on, we can accept them as the necessary garb for the characters, whereas if the characters come on the stage fully costumed, we think at once of the work of the director and the costume designer. The effect Genet achieves here by the metatheatrical device of having us present at the dressing up of his personages is akin to certain characteristic effects of Pirandello. I am thinking, for example, of the scene in *Tonight We Improvise*, in which an old man rehearses his death-scene; here Pirandello is able to touch us with the feeling of the real imminence of death in a way he never would have been able to do by showing us a man really dying. We tend to think of real blood on the stage as a fake; now the magic of metatheatre can make stage blood seem real; at least we can think of it as real for a moment and without feeling that we have been taken in.

Outside the brothel a revolution is taking place. In a remarkable scene, the revolutionaries discuss a bit of theatre designed to impose their aims on the populace. Should they not make of Chantal, a prostitute from Madame Irma's "Palace of Illusions," a saint of their revolution? If they were to kill her and claim that she fell as a martyr to their cause, would not her image impel the people to victory? But what good is our victory if come by that way, protests one of the revolutionaries, "it already has a dose of clap." The point is made that the revolutionaries must make a determined effort to do without illusion. Perhaps they can. "Have they jumped into reality?" asks the Police Chief from his headquarters in Madame Irma's brothel. Evidently the real adversary of the revolution is none other than Madame Irma. Moreover, she has already conquered. The revolutionaries will not be able to remain real; what is more, they do not want to. They may conquer the palace, the legislature, the army, the courts; they will not be able to control the old whorehouses.

It is the revolutionaries in Genet's play who represent implacable values. Actually, in the modern world, only revolutionaries have been able to represent such values. Hence, the prestige of revolutionaries. But Genet has taken their measure too and finally renders them ridiculous. We have the impression that they will all come finally to Madame Irma's Balcony. They are would-be tragedians in the world of metatheatre.

Yet in a way Genet shares the weakness of his revolutionaries in The Balcony; he too would like to create something other than the kind of play he can make so magnificently; this master of the metaplay would like to create tragedy. And the sentimental inclination toward something impossible for him is responsible, I believe, for the one bad scene in The Balcony, a scene almost fatal to the second half of the play, lasting for almost an hour and boring from beginning to end. Having absorbed the revolution with its insistence on reality into the illusionist world of The Great Balcony, Genet suddenly reverses himself and tries to see illusion itself as inexorable. But this is an impossible idea, contrary to all dramatic judgment or good sense: it may be our fate to have illusions; this does not mean that illusion can have the same force as fate. Or to put the matter better, fate might free us from illusions, but is probably itself illusory. This is more or less what Genet has said throughout his play, but at the very end he seems to want to say the contrary. I noted this weakness in another play of his, *The Maids*. It was not necessary for one of the two girls actually to take poison in that work, since when she did I felt that she was acting. There is something similar in *The Balcony* at the very close. The Chief of Police wants to be apotheosized and as a phallus. He achieves this grandiose aim when a client (none other than the very revolutionary who had wanted to keep the revolution real), pretending to be the Chief of Police, castrates himself. The episode is brutal, vulgar, and utterly undramatic. Should illusion also have sacrifices, martyrs? I explain the weak thinking here as not peculiar to Genet but present in modern intellectuals. They are afraid of the implications of their own ideas, which have rendered the world less real than they would like it to be. They do not want to think of life as a dream, but as serious, valid, overwhelming maybe. They would like nothing better than to come upon some implacable value they could regard as true. So the one real fault in Genet's play is not just his. We all have some share in it. Yet, in the main, the point of view of Genet is that the destruction of illusion, as represented by *The Balcony*, would be the destruction of life as such. Is this thought shocking? Some of the reviewers evidently thought so. But is the French dramatist's view really so different from that expressed by Prospero at the conclusion of *The Tempest*? If anything, I should say that Genet's play ends less cynically than Shakespeare's. For Genet the revels have not ended. The action will continue. The more or less humble characters will again mount on stilts and costume themselves to be again extravagant in sex. Illusion and reality cannot be segregated; they will continually change places, and be the Same to the Other, the Other to the Same.

My contention is that the dramatic philosophy of *The Balcony*, as of Genet's *The Maids*, and of his play *The Blacks*, while certainly his own, is yet, when we think of it formally, the same dramatic philosophy present in *Twelfth Night, Measure for Measure, Hamlet, The Tempest, Life Is a Dream.* Let none then reproach Jean Genet for his ideas. His thought proceeds on a level where one can only think what has to be thought. Without tragedy, of which we may be incapable, there is no philosophic alternative to the two concepts by which I have defined the metaplay: the world is a stage, life is a dream.

Beckett and Metatheatre

I LINK BECKETT with Genet because the plays of both are modern works of metatheatre. Beckett's metatheatre is very special. His plays almost never present a play-within-a-play sequence. And his characters, although imaginative creations, have a kind of sad naturalness. Their physical oddities, inflictions, and illnesses are exhibited; they wheeze, they whine, they groan or sigh unguardedly, as people do in real life. James Joyce, who in his writings never overlooked human infirmities, no doubt influenced Beckett to describe people naturalistically. All the same, Beckett's plays are very far from realism. How does he get his strange effects?

Every one of Beckett's plays suggests that some decisive action has gone on before the characters have come into our view. Take Beckett's two principal works, *Waiting for Godot* and *Endgame.* The characters in these plays, Estragon and Vladimir, Pozzo and Lucky, Hamm and Clov, Nagg and Nell, are made dramatic, not so much by what they do as by what has already happened to them. They show us the results of dramatic action, but not that action itself. Their drama consists in having been capable of drama at some time, and in their remembrance of that time. On the stage, they remember that once they had a stage for their thoughts, feelings, and better bodies.

All of Beckett's plays are epilogues and hence contracted. His people are people who have dwindled, as a result of what they did or what was done to them. Moreover, all that is left for them to do, as we catch sight of them, is to play. And the action, insofar as there is action in any play of Beckett's, consists precisely in playing. Estragon's life with Vladimir is a series of scenes they put on to while away the time. Certainly Pozzo and Lucky have nothing particular to do; Pozzo's only possible action is to exhibit Lucky's tricks as a theatre manager might put on those of an acrobat or a freak. In *Endgame*, all that is left for Hamm and Clov is to play, but without joy. Here is one of Beckett's strongest dramatic effects. In *Krapp's Last Tape*, the protagonist, who is also the only person on the stage, plays with himself. If this sounds masturbatory, then I have not been misunderstood. As a matter of fact, Krapp's eating of a banana is done in such a way—and Beckett's stage directions are very precise—as to give just this suggestion. Moreover, Krapp plays with his tapes, on which his memories are transcribed. He plays with his memories, too—all writers do that—but Krapp does it without any aim or purpose. What has happened to him? This we are not told. Perhaps nothing much more than that time has passed. But the passage of time, however slow it may seem, however gently said our farewells to each particular moment, is drastic in the extreme. Time brings infirmity and death closer; it effaces the thrill of past enjoyment. As an individual's past time increases, the future time left him dwindles. It is at this moment that an individual becomes interesting to Beckett, and worth setting on the stage.

In *All That Fall* there is a definite and simple action. An infirm, old woman, weary and wheezing, struggles to the station to meet her blind husband and take him home with her. But the real event is not in the action presented; rather, through this action the real event is indicated: what time has done to both the woman and her husband. We see their different infirmities, caused by the same enemy of both—time. Weakness, tiredness, blindness, lameness, deafness, oldness—these are its effects.

In Beckett's most recent play, *Happy Days*, he presents a woman buried in the ground to her waist. Just as much of her is gone as is present when the curtain rises. The action of the play consists in her sinking deeper into the ground, so that when the curtain falls, only her head is visible. In the meantime, there is nothing for her to do but to recall what is absent from the stage and to play with her husband, who circles about her on all fours. Is he like a dog on the scent, trying to find the trail of all that is gone?

Why are time and its effects so important to Beckett? Because, I suspect, of his nostalgia for eternity. Should we not be, at the very least, the playthings of eternity and not merely the playthings of time? Such is the question Beckett poses in his plays, thus suggesting that the actual characters are themselves the scenes of an invisible action: the action of time, which might be eternal itself, or the surrogate, although we cannot be sure of this, for eternity.

But these plays cannot be understood or appreciated fully unless we recognize that for all their special content, oddity, and purely personal lyricism, they conform to the kind of dramatic work I have designated as metatheatre: what makes them so special is that life in these plays has been theatricalized, not by any attitudes taken by the characters, not by any tricks of dramaturgy, and not by the author's intent to demonstrate any propositions about the world, but by the mere passage of time, that drastic fact of ordinary life.

But we should expect in metatheatrical works some element of metaphysical wonder; and there is that in Beckett's plays. Who is the real enemy of Vladimir, Estragon, Lucky, Pozzo? Of the characters of *Endgame, All That Fall, Krapp's Last Tape,* and *Happy Days?* Who is their enemy? If the author knew for sure, he would have told us in works of didactic character; he would not have played with his doubts and fancies, nor would he have presented characters who do little other than play. He would have written works with a thesis, not pieces of metatheatre.

Brecht: His Nay and His Yea

OF DEVIOUS BERT BRECHT

I THINK it was Herbert Luethy who first pointed up the many ambiguities of Brecht's career and character.* As Luethy saw him, Brecht the moralist was also Brecht the cynic; Brecht the propagandist of revolutionary terror was also Brecht the temperamentally passive and sly opportunist; Brecht the committed Communist was also Brecht the self-serving literary maneuverer, who managed by cunning and compromise to foist his formalist theatre on a Communist world opposed to most of his theories. Luethy describes the playwright after his return to Germany, sitting in East Berlin:

. . . surrounded by the secret odor of heresy, sedition, decadence, formalism, and objectivism, tolerated for his propaganda value and gently scolded for his willfullness—and armed, moreover, with the Austrian citizenship he foresightedly acquired, as well as with dollar contracts and Western publishing rights. So he sits, splendid and well organized, on the very outermost limb of the free world—busily sawing it through.

Eric Bentley, however, has looked more favorably on Brecht's ambiguities, interpreting these as signs of a broad and complex nature, stirred by diverse, if conflicting, interests.† Moreover Bentley takes direct issue with Luethy's suggested division of Brecht's career into two parts. Bentley protests:

To Mr. Luethy, the early Brecht is a good thing, the later a bad, just as to many Communists and fellow-travelers, the early Brecht is a bad thing, the later a good.

It would be strange indeed if a poet could cut his creative life so neatly in half. I believe that one can only get the impression that Brecht did so if one is blinded by political prejudice. If

* "Of Poor Bert Brecht" by Herbert Luethy, *Encounter*, July 1956.
† Eric Bentley's introduction to *Seven Plays by Bertolt Brecht*. Grove Press.

Brecht had a divided nature, it was—as the word *nature* implies —divided all his life long. Such a division is discernible in every major play.

I take it that if there were two Brechts at different points of the playwright's career, one "bad" and the other "good," we would be able to reject the "bad" Brecht altogether and keep the "good" Brecht intact. But if Brecht was "divided all his life long," we have no alternative, since we admire the artist, but to accept him in all his ambiguousness.

Brecht was devious but Bentley is indulgent. Not so Martin Esslin, whose study of the playwright is awed, fervent, worshipful. Esslin ends up his very knowledgeable and certainly valuable book* with an eloquent—and I think too pat—list of the many ways in which Brecht's efforts defeated his peculiar ends:

He wanted to be a writer for the common people, as easy to understand as fair-ground comedians, but the more simple he tried to be, the more complex his work became, so that only intellectuals could appreciate it; he wanted to serve the cause of the revolution, but was regarded with suspicion by its recognized standard bearers, who reviled him as a formalist and banned him as a dangerous, defeatist influence; he wanted to arouse the critical faculties of his audience, but only succeeded in moving them to tears; he wanted to make his theatre a laboratory of social change, a living proof that the world and mankind could be altered, and had to see it strengthen the public's faith in the enduring virtues of unchanging human nature. He had to witness his villains acclaimed as heroes and his heroes mistaken for villains. He sought to spread the cold light of logical clarity—and produced a rich texture of poetic ambiguity. He abhorred the very idea of beauty—and created beauty.

Ronald Gray† is much less interested in the man Brecht who "abhorred beauty"—if indeed he did—than in the playwright Brecht who created beauty. But this critic tells us that Brecht's plays are ambiguous in the extreme, most particularly the last plays of his greatest period. The protagonists of these works—Puntilla, Courage, Azdak, and Galileo— are all morally divided beings, and to appreciate them we

* *Brecht,* by Martin Esslin. Doubleday Anchor Books.
† *Bertolt Brecht,* by Ronald Gray. Grove Press. A very well-informed and often penetrating study of Brecht's productions, theories, and plays.

must divide our moral judgment; we have to condemn these characters even as we approve them: they are too complex to be merely admired or blamed.

Now I find it hard to believe that Brecht and his work are as ambiguous as the critics claim. If they are right, then would his work be admirable? A great contribution in art is always an effort toward simplification, and ambiguity—in a work or a life—is only a sign of richness, when not a final datum. Moreover, Brecht's plays, on my reading of them, have a definiteness, hardness, and clarity which testify to a single vision, to a determined will, to an idea. Now there is no idea that is not luminous. To be sure, Brecht's plays have a grayness that is characteristically his, but unquestionably they have also a Brechtian vividness, a Brechtian clarity.

Is it not at least theoretically possible that the critics of Brecht so far have been too easily satisfied with disparaging, justifying, or extolling the playwright's ambiguities, taken as ultimate? May there not after all be some definite, unequivocal conviction in Brecht's life and work?

I want to propose these simple—and I hope simplifying —questions: Is there any value that Brecht denied consistently, perseveringly, profoundly? Is there any value that Brecht affirmed unyieldingly with all his force and with all his cunning, again and again? Was there a real Nay in him? An authentic Yea?

BRECHT'S NAY

If Brecht were merely a nay sayer our inquiry would be quickly ended. What Brecht denied in his early poems and in his first play, *Baal*—written when he was twenty-one— Brecht continued to deny with more or less vehemence and subtlety throughout all of his work, in one play after another.

Baal is raucous, exuberant, and at times exquisite; in it, Brecht announces once and for all the object of his enduring hatred, contempt, and disbelief: the individual, that is to say, moral experience. Herbert Luethy says of *Baal*: "Here is everything one could wish for in the way of mockery of religion, of humanity, of simple morality." True enough but I think not quite precise. A deeper statement was made about it in the early twenties by the Viennese poet Hugo von Hofmannsthal, one of Brecht's earliest admirers, who wrote a dramatic prologue for an experimental production of the play in Vienna. In this prologue the spokesman for the new drama says:

Our time is unredeemed; and do you know what it wants to be redeemed from? . . . The individual . . . Our age groans too heavily under the weight of this child of the sixteenth century that the nineteenth fed to monstrous size . . . We are anonymous forces. Potentialities of the soul. Individuality is an arabesque we have discarded. . . . I should go so far as to assert that all the ominous events we have been witnessing in the last twelve years are nothing but a very awkward and longwinded way of burying the concept of the European individual in the grave it has dug for itself. . . .

These are fateful words, and they tell us a great deal not only about Brecht, but about the whole epoch. If indeed the European concept of the individual was burying itself in the grave it had dug for itself, if this was the truth about the time—in Brecht's judgment of it, as well as in Hofmannsthal's—then surely moral experience was meaningless, moral suffering absurd, morality was, in Rimbaud's phrase, "a weakness of the brain." I think Brecht never deviated from this view. This is why he was from the start opposed to tragedy—an impossible form if one did not take moral sufferings seriously—and also opposed to realism, the theatrical form inherited from Ibsen in which the individual plays so large a role. In *A Man's a Man* Brecht expressed his hatred for the individual analytically, dramatizing the process by which a so-called individual is rid of his original identity and a brand new one, more serviceable to others, is installed in him. In *Three Penny Opera* Brecht had musicalized his basic negation; in this farcial and boisterous extravaganza, moral experience is ridiculed and all positive values are buried to the wonderful jazz music Brecht had inspired Kurt Weill to write. How striking this work must have been to Berlin audiences in the Depression of 1929 may be gauged if we consider the tonic and shocking effect of Jack Gelber's play *The Connection* on New York audiences in 1960. In Gelber's play, square values are

buried to the newest music: in Brecht's ever-so-much
stronger work, all moral values—courage, loyalty, honesty,
and charity—are swept away to a music that is overwhelming. The high point of the play is reached when
MacHeath's girl, Jenny the Whore, invokes the black ship
whose armed men—that is her dream—will descend on the
city and ask her whom to kill. Her answer: "Everyone."

Brecht's play was produced a few years before Hitler's
assumption of power; but the signs of coming catastrophe
were evident. Writers in Germany and elsewhere who had
toyed more superficially with nihilism began to recant such
views, and look for positive values to stay them in the
coming storm. This was the period when intellectuals were
converted to Catholicism, also to Communism. Brecht,
too, must have felt the need for positive affirmation. In
fact, a year before the production of *Three Penny Opera*,
he elected to support the German Communist Party, but
in so doing he in no way took back his original negation.
Communism for Brecht was still another way of denying
the individual, and the value of moral experience as such.

YEA BUT NOT QUITE

Shortly after *Three Penny Opera*, Brecht wrote a little
play, *The Measures Taken*, which was performed in Berlin
in 1930. This play is certainly a masterpiece; and in its great
virtues and characteristic defects reveals what Brecht would
have liked dogmatic Communism to mean to him; Communism would not have that meaning to him for long.

The Measures Taken is a kind of abstract and speculative
exercise in the experience of total commitment. Four Communist agitators who had been sent into China by the Communist Party report to the Control Commission on what
they have achieved. They have little to show for their
efforts other than the murder of a young agitator who,
utterly devoted to revolutionary work, was judged unfit for
such work by them. Apparently he hampered them in their
revolutionary efforts by the too great value he set on his
moral feelings. They liquidated the young man not because
of any counterrevolutionary initiative on his part, but
simply because he was an individual, hence an encum-

brance to the Party. For, as the Leader at Party headquarters has told them—and this is the moral of the play—
agitators are to be nameless and motherless, blank pages
on which the revolution writes its instructions. The Control chorus commends the four agitators for their action.
After all, even the best individual is limited. And the
Control chorus sings in praise of the Party:

> A single man has two eyes
> The Party has a thousand eyes
> The Party sees seven states
> A single man sees one city
> A single man has a single hour
> But the Party has many hours
> A single man can be annihilated
> But the Party cannot be annihilated
> For it is the advance guard of the masses
> And conducts its struggle
> By the methods described in the classics which were created
> From acquaintance with reality.*

What is denied in this play is what Brecht had always
denied: the individual, moral experience as such. What is
affirmed in the play is something new for Brecht: the absolute authority of the Party bureaucracy.

From the response of the Communists to *The Measures
Taken*, Brecht was to learn something about the Party
bureaucracy he had not taken into account when he wrote
his play: the Party, while it wanted to be treated as an
absolute, did not want its pretensions to absoluteness ex-
posed—or even justified. According to Martin Esslin:

The Party was horrified that Brecht had given the anti-Com-
munist press the occasion of speaking about the "murderous
practices" of the Communist Party, and the Party organs
strenuously denied that any such killing could ever happen in
reality. *Die Linkskurve* attacked Brecht's lack of revolutionary
experience: "One feels that he does not draw his knowledge
from practice, that he is merely deducing from theory. . . .
The unreal analysis of the premises leads to a false synthesis
of their political and artistic consequences. All this mirrors an
abstract attitude toward the manifold and complicated store of
knowledge, derived from experience, which the party possesses."

* Eric Bentley's translation of *The Measures Taken*. See his an-
thology, *The Modern Theatre Volume 6*. Doubleday Anchor
Book.

In the light of these criticisms Brecht revised the text. But the second performance still did not satisfy the critics. The *Rote Fahne* admonished him: "The author of *The Measures Taken*, Bert Brecht, must be told that knowledge of the theories of Marxism-Leninism is not enough, that the genius and wide reading of a writer cannot take the place of revolutionary experience and detailed day-to-day work in the movement."

Brecht remained politically loyal to the Party and did not break with it, but his attitude toward it must have changed, even if there is no evidence that it did immediately. To have written a work which cannot be performed for any audience—*The Measures Taken* was too pro-Communist for Communists, hence for anti-Communists —cannot but have the meaning to the dramatist of some fundamental failing in his conception. Moreover, though brilliant, Brecht's play was on the other hand arid and abstract—"icily inhuman," Luethy has called it—and in it there was little possibility for satisfying the feeling for concreteness, sensation, naturalness, and ecstasy that Brecht had been able to express in his early poetry and in his first play, *Baal*.

Brecht never again attempted to present the Party as an absolute value in a dramatic work. Is it so strange or paradoxical then that while remaining a Communist he would in the future protect himself, his rights, freedom, money, and literary works from Communist Party control? Why should he have treated as absolute in fact what he could not celebrate imaginatively as absolute? So Brecht's behavior toward the Communists during his exile and after he returned to East Germany, a behavior Luethy regards as so ambiguous, seems to me not to be ambiguous in the least. If there is any paradox in Brecht's relations with the Communists from this point on, I think that paradox belongs to Communism and not to Bertolt Brecht.

YEA, VERILY!

The first signs of what Brecht was to affirm finally appear in a little play written in 1934, which has the additional interest of being based on a seventeenth-century masterpiece from which Brecht took the fable for his own work. Brecht's play *The Horations and the Curiations* is a kind

of parody of Corneille's *Horace*. The latter work, still taught
in the French lycées as one of the five great tragedies of
Corneille, tells the story of how the three Horations fought
the three Curiations, the latter representing Alba; the Horations, Rome. From this struggle only one of the Horations
emerged; his two brothers are slain. He himself has killed
the three champions of Alba. Now he has a sister, who is
the wife of one of the three Curiations. When she hears
the result of the conflict, she denounces her brother and
Rome. Whereupon the patriotic hero kills her. Whatever
one thinks finally of this extravagant and I believe over-
praised tragedy—it is not truly tragic—it was an effort to
present an individual on a scale as large and as significant
as the Rome with which he is identified.

Let us look now at what Brecht did with the same story.
In his play the issue between the two cities is not one of
honor but one of economics, and the struggle of the three
Curiation brothers with the three Horations is described
in entirely physical terms without any relation either to
ideals or feelings. The three champions on each side are
urged to do battle by Choruses representing the people of
Alba and of Rome. Here is a typically Brechtian touch: the
first of the three Horations, on his first appearance, is presented with a bow, which he bends but not to the full. He
says: "I could bend it more, but it would break." The
Chorus replies: "Try to make the most of it, we have no
other bow for you." Horatius: "Its range will be too short."
Chorus: "You'll have to move closer to your enemy."
Horatius: "But then I'll be a better target for him." Chorus:
"Naturally." The battle proceeds. It is told purely in terms
of the use each champion is able to make of his material
situation and the weapon at his disposal. The final victory
comes to the Horation who makes shrewder use of his pos-
sibilities of action than do his opponents. When the three
Curiations, having killed two of the Horations, converge on
the sole remaining champion of Rome, the latter, by running
away, manages to separate his three opponents, then turns
around and kills each of them in turn.

(Is not Brecht's way of treating the conflict between
Alba and Rome, each represented by three brothers, in
many ways prophetic of the struggle for prestige now

going on between the Soviet Union and the United States, in which each of the great powers is represented by its cosmonauts? Also there is the very Brechtian fact that the richer power, America, has the poorer spaceships for its champions. Moreover, the manner in which the great adventure in space is being conducted by selected teams of the two powers provides a striking illustration of the diminishment of the individual, as a direct consequence of technological and collective achievement. If we compare Columbus' crossing of the Atlantic to Lindbergh's flight certainly the first crossing was the greater act, requiring far greater imagination and a stronger will. But Lindbergh's flight in its turn was still the act of an individual, whereas the magnificent present-day flights into space and outside gravity are only made possible by teams of experts and by precision instruments. Our present-day heroes are individuals trained to adjust themselves to function like machines.)

Corneille's play was a celebration of individual heroism and will. Brecht's is the celebration of animal dexterity, animal courage, animal cunning. Corneille's Horatius, victor over the three Curiations against whom he had not the slightest personal animosity and one of whom was his own brother-in-law, guilty, too, of his sister's murder, is a frightening and grotesque image of individual greatness. Brecht's Horation, wounded and limping, covered with his own blood and also that of the enemies he has killed, is an image of the cornered human animal, emerging from a situation from which he has had the luck to escape alive. The hero of Corneille's play is the individual soul. The hero of Brecht's play is the human body.

Moreover it is the human body which is the hero of every important play Brecht wrote from then on. The human body in its desire to feed, sustain, and expend itself is the real hero of *Mother Courage, Puntilla, The Caucasian Chalk Circle,* and of *Galileo.* I think it was Brecht's adoration of the body which made it possible for him to view optimistically the decline and death of the individual and even to celebrate it poetically. The ambiguities seen by critics in the main characters of the plays mentioned disappear when it is recognized that Brecht was interested neither in condemning his characters nor in justifying them, though at times it must be admitted he implied he was. When we read the plays carefully we note what the critics have already noted, that the main characters are morally incoherent. But their moral incoherence simply means, I suggest, that Brecht was not interested in them as individuals, but as striking images of the human body in its assertiveness, natural ecstasy, and desire to endure.

Take *Puntilla*. The question raised about this wonderful folk comedy is whether the main figure, Puntilla, a Finnish landowner, was intended as a positive or as a negative character. He is a negative character when he is sober. For at such times he is grasping, avaricious, a tyrant over his servants and farmhands; when sober he plans to marry his daughter to a government official whom she does not love and whom Puntilla himself despises, and to marry himself to a wealthy widow he cannot abide. But when Puntilla is drunk, he is quite another man: he treats his servants as equals, urges his chauffeur in fact to marry his daughter, and proposes to every girl he meets, no matter what her class. When drunk Puntilla is generous, natural, large-minded, and amiable. This is because he is under the influence of his body. A great moment of the play: Puntilla, dead drunk, urinates ecstatically with his chauffeur against a wall. He says:

I couldn't live in the city. I need the open air, I have to piss freely under the stars. If I can't have that, what have I? They say that to do this outdoors is primitive. But I think it primitive to piss on tile . . . I want people to enjoy life. I want those who work for me to learn how to be gay. It disgusts me to see a man, his head down, just dragging along. . . .

Puntilla would like to combine his consciousness when sober with his gaiety when drunk. This of course is impossible. But there can be no doubt at all that it is not Puntilla sober whom Brecht wants us to accept. Puntilla drunk is, to be sure, something less than an individual. He is also something more.

The protagonist of *Mother Courage,* the canteen woman who makes a living out of the Thirty Years' War has also raised similar difficulties for critics, apparently even for Brecht himself. Luethy finds her utterly positive:

Completely authentic in particular is the splendid figure of
Mother Courage, the army camp *vivandière*, with her covered
wagon and her three children begotten by different fathers from
among the various nations of Europe: endlessly on the move
through the endless war, haggling and cursing, swindling and
victimized, grimly, bravely, and vainly defending her brood
against seducers, press gangs, and execution squads. She is a
small shareholder in the murderous business of war; she is
nourished by the slaughter and at the same time condemned
to pay the price—by sacrificing her children, one after the
other. Twelve years of this unequal struggle pass across the
stage, and in the final scene she is alone, while the war con-
tinues: and with her lonely wagon she follows the trail of destruction through the devastated land, on the heels of ragged
armies of mercenaries—Imperial, Swedish Lutheran, Catholic:
who cares: War is war.

Against this view Eric Bentley protests:

His [Brecht's] protagonists are nothing if not *negative* heroes.
Brecht got angry when actresses made Courage noble and even
—supreme error!—courageous.

And Ronald Gray notes:

At its simplest level *Mother Courage* is an antiwar play, de-
nouncing the stupidity of its central characters who live by the
war and yet are blind to the penalties it brings. So important
was this to Brecht that, when he found his "bourgois" audiences
at the first performances in Zurich sympathizing with Mother
Courage, admiring her tenacity in the face of adversity, he
rewrote or modified several passages, supplying baser motives
for her actions and emphasizing . . . her inhumanity.

Gray suggests that, as with Puntilla, "Brecht did not intend
Mother Courage to be either only praised or only condemned."

So the critics do not agree as to how Courage should
be taken. Nor apparently did Brecht agree with the effect
his play evoked when performed. How are we to take
Courage then? Certainly, we are not to approve her morally.
But the affecting thing about her is not her moral consciousness but her vitality, her physical endurance, her ability to
go on from horror to horror, her unabatable animality. All
the confusions about her character arise from the error
of considering her as an individual, with a moral consciousness of a sort we must condemn or approve. She is

not that at all. Her consciousness is as incoherent as Puntilla's desire to be sober and drunk at the same time, and enjoy the advantages of both. Yet Courage is not a negative figure; her positive attributes are those of the body, not of the soul.

The *Caucasian Chalk Circle* is a delightful play, treating in a most sophisticated way of simple folk. And it has a great character—one of the most wonderful Brecht ever set on the stage. This is Azdak who at the play's end as the presiding judge decides that Grusha, whom we have come to love and admire, is the rightful mother of the boy she has raised since an infant and for whom she has even married a corpse (though it turns out that the corpse is not really dead; in any case the marriage ceremony in which Grusha is wedded to what she takes to be the corpse of Simon is one of the best scenes in modern theatre). Azdak's decision goes against the claim of the boy's natural mother (who has never suffered over his upbringing and only desires him in order to have legal rights over her estate). Azdak, who makes what we think the right decision, does so for reasons we cannot formulate. He is himself a thief, an opportunist, a coward, and a rogue; but he is always unpredictable; after he allows the Grand Duke to escape he promptly goes to the authorities and denounces himself, no one can say why. All of his decisions have the suddenness and strangeness of some new association, as in dreams. Why does he do this rather than that? This is like asking why during the night one suddenly prefers to sleep on the other side. Azdak's consciousness, if one can even call it consciousness, is as close to that penumbra between the soul and the body as consciousness can be; everything he says or does has a kind of bodily charm. I think there never has been anyone quite like him on the stage.

Yet Eric Bentley reports that when he talked with Bertolt Brecht the latter had said that Ernest Busch, in his performance as Azdak, had missed the "whole tragic side of the role." Coming from Brecht and on the topic of Azdak, the remark could not fail to strike Bentley. Here is his comment:

. . . Brecht usually talked *against* tragedy, and those who have found "a tragic side" in his work have assumed that he was unconscious of it. What *is* tragic about Azdak? On the surface, the part is all racy and ironic comedy. But, aside from anything he says, Azdak performs an action near the beginning of his part of the play which casts a good deal of light on the whole: *having let the Grand Duke escape, he denounces himself to the authorities for so doing.* It is a very bizarre incident, in itself hard to believe, and, as acted by Busch, flatly incredible. What is its moral and psychological content? First, self-denunciation, as often in Brecht and Communist culture generally, is seen as a good. . . . Second, the "goodness" is canceled by the fact that the authorities surrendered to are bad. The tragedy of Azdak, as found in this incident, is that his effort at heroism is reduced to absurdity by the cricumstances. . . . *The tragedy of Azdak is that his life is a comedy.*

One must be grateful to Bentley for this information about Brecht, and Bentley's concluding point is the very one I would make, though I would express the matter differently. If Azdak, according to Brecht, is tragic, this is because he cannot suffer morally, he is not an individual; that I assume is what Bentley means in saying that Azdak is tragic insofar as his life is a "comedy." Brecht's comment on his own character reveals that the playwright, who had so radically denied moral experience, was admitting that this very denial did not go without moral suffering. . . .

But most extraordinary of all Brecht's poetical celebrations of the body is his play *Galileo,* which treats one of the great representatives of Western science. Brecht's play, quietly told in scenes wherein the dramatic conflicts are always understated and never pushed too far, describes the physicist in relation to his own ideas, to rival theorists, to his daughter, to his disciple, and to the Church. In the main the play concentrates on the motives that led Galileo to deny his own theory about the movement of the earth and his recantation of his recantation to his disciple afterward. The play is never really exciting nor does it rise to any great emotional height. One never feels that any tremendous issue is at stake. But it has a wonderful movement, an intellectual beauty, and the figure of the great Galileo charms utterly. This is one of Brecht's best plays, perhaps his greatest.

It has been said that Brecht himself regarded his pro-

tagonist, Galileo, as a criminal for yielding to the pressure
of the Church, and that Brecht wanted audiences to condemn him for his cowardice. Apparently he thought that
science had suffered from Galileo's recantation, and hence
that Galileo was a criminal for not enduring martyrdom.
Indeed the English critic Harold Hobson, interpreting
Brecht's intention, goes even further:

The point of *Galileo* is that men do not today live in an age
of Reason simply because at a particular moment in the seven-
teenth century Galileo recanted before the Inquisition. As in
one view humanity is saved by the Grace and death of Christ,
so, in Brecht's, by the life and disgrace of Galileo, humanity
is damned. Galileo is nothing more or less than Brecht's anti-
Christ. He is the God who failed us.

Now I do not think this is the point of *Galileo* at all,
even if Brecht thought it was. First of all there is the dramatic fact of Galileo's great and invincible charm. It is
one thing for him to condemn his own behavior, to accuse
himself of cowardice, and it is another thing for an audience to join in so judging him. Moreover the cause of
science was not set back by Galileo's recantation. The great
scientist could very well have calculated that since his
theory was true, in time it would come to be accepted—
even by the Church—as has been in fact the case. If Brecht
thought that Galileo should have undergone martyrdom,
then his thinking can be called gross. Nietzsche and Kierkegaard both remarked that martyrdom is unjustifiable except
in the name of something whose victory is uncertain: it is
not really martyrdom to die for the sake of something you
know will succeed.

Here again we have a case of what seems to be an insurmountable ambiguity in one of Brecht's main characters,
an ambiguity so deep that Brecht himself was never able
to explain it satisfactorily or justify it. What are we to
think of Galileo? The same question has already been
asked about Puntilla, Mother Courage, and Azdak. Bentley thinks we ought to look upon Galileo as an artist, as a
man who is both a genius and a rogue.

Now I do not think this a satisfactory judgment at all.

If Brecht had wanted to describe an artist, why did he choose to dramatize the life of a scientist?

Very revealing of Brecht's intention is the interest he showed in the physical presentation of his play. For instance, Brecht approved Charles Laughton's way of expounding the Ptolemaic and Copernican systems while taking his morning wash, stripped to the waist. According to Ronald Gray, this was because "Galileo's pleasure here was not merely intellectual, but physical also, in fact his appetite for knowledge has to be shown as part of his appetite for all things." And Brecht himself has remarked of Laughton's performance:

And the movements of his hands in his trouser pockets, when he was planning new researches were all but scandalous. Whenever Galileo was being creative, Laughton revealed a contradictory mixture of aggressiveness and defenseless softness and sensitivity.

The text bears out this characteristic insight of Brecht's. For Galileo is shown as a man interested in eating, drinking, and thinking. Someone says of him, "He has thinking bouts." Thought is reduced to a physical activity. And Galileo says: "I don't understand a man who doesn't use his mind to fill his belly." The mind according to Galileo ought to serve the body, in the instance cited—the belly. So consistently in fact has Brecht physicalized Galileo's intelligence that one begins to wonder after a while whether even the word *mind,* with its hint of spirituality, is proper when applied to the great scientist.

The paradoxes and ambiguities of Galileo's character disappear, I suggest, when we think of the great figure in the play *not* as a representative of human spirit at all or of mind either, except in terms of its physical seat, the brain. The remarkable daring of this play, still I think not fully appreciated by critics, is that in it Brecht took one of the greatest scientists of the West and made of him, like of the landowner Puntilla, the thief and scoundrel Azdak, the canteen woman Courage, a representative of the human body—in Galileo's case, a representative of the body in its most intellectual posture, but still at a very far remove from what we can very properly call spirit or even mind.

OF BERT BRECHT—NOT SIMPLE BUT SIMPLIFIED

If the judgments I have made are valid—I have based them on the same facts presented by Brecht's critics—then surely it is possible to see, beyond the playwright's ambiguities, not to be explained away, a Brecht rather impressive in his consistency. He began by denying moral experience and the individual—not I think out of indifference, but moved by rage and disappointment by the discovery that in his time the very idea of the European individual was dying, burying itself, in Hofmannsthal's words, "in the grave it dug for itself." It is to be noted that a similar conviction about the individual is discoverable in the works of Western writers before and during Brecht's time. What but the judgment that the individual was dead or dying lies behind Eliot's suspicion of individual insight, Joyce's cult of impersonality, the surrealist's dependence on automatic writing, Lawrence's assertion that he was not interested in describing individuals, but only psychic and biological forces? Brecht of course denied the individual more radically than anyone else and maintained this negation throughout his life. This does not mean, however, that we should judge him a moral cynic.

But if Brecht denied moral experience, can he be called a moralist? This is a more complicated matter; but one point has to be made strongly. Brecht was not, except for a short period in his career, the moralist of commitment to Communist Party authority. It is true that he wrote *The Measures Taken*. And Sidney Hook tells this story about Brecht: In New York, during the preparation of one of the Moscow trials, Brecht was asked by Hook if he thought the accused in Moscow were guilty or innocent. Brecht replied cryptically: "If they are innocent they ought to be shot." Hook, telling the story with great moral heat, accuses Brecht of being an antihumanist. But Brecht never claimed to be a humanist. He had never affirmed the individual; I think he never believed the individual in this society could be quite real or that moral experience could be anything but an imposture. Hence, what difference did it make whether the accused in Moscow were innocent or guilty? He was not going to fight against the Soviet State in the name of something he thought an anachronism. If he was a moralist at all, then it was in a stern refusal to regard moral experience positively—and so uncompromising a refusal does have a moral side. (One thinks of Brecht's saying that Azdak has a tragic side.)

What Brecht affirmed was the body, the human body in its warmth, its weakness, its susceptibility, its appetites, the human body in its longing and in its thought. Why did he remain a Communist? He may have thought that even distorted modern Communism, because of its philosophical basis in materialism, was the politics of the human body and hence preferable to Western liberalism based on what he considered a false affirmation of the individual soul.

It may be that his interest in the body extended itself to an interest in the physical details of his own productions, in the material and circumstantial values his plays could have, in their bodies, so to speak, as against their written dialogue, which we may not incorrectly think of as a play's soul. The attention other playwrights have given to the literary form of their plays Brecht devoted indefatigably to the details of his productions. Writers have been honored for their conscientious search for the right word. Brecht was utterly conscientious in his search for the right stage business to bring out the strongest meanings of his plays.

I think of Brecht as somehow the opposite of Webster, with whom the great period of Elizabethan drama came to a close. Webster placed on the stage characters of tremendous will and ruthless energies, aristocrats, marvelously appareled. They live in palaces and plot continuously against each other. Though not noble in the moral sense they are highly spiritual, refined even in their cruelties, and invariably they are betrayed. By what? By their bodies. Under the fine garments, the bodies that bear their violent wills are destructible, susceptible to decay and to death. The power of the human will belied by the weakness of the body which is its seat, such is the theme of Webster's meditation, of his grandiose eloquence.

And in Brecht we have the very reverse. The best of his characters are mainly passive, morally inconsequential, or inconsistent. They live by lies, by fraud, and if, on occasion by feats of thought, the thought generally ministers to their bodies. I think Brecht loved the body, in the abstract, of course, with a feeling similar to what each person feels for his own.

To make the body his hero, Brecht of course had to make use of a very particular dramatic method and rely on a special form.

Brecht and Metatheatre

I

How DID BRECHT come to metatheatre?

In analyzing Brecht's values,* I showed that from the very start of his career as a playwright he rejected the individual and moral experience, so important in the realistic European drama as it was shaped by Ibsen, and in Germany continued by Hauptmann and Sudermann. For Brecht these playwrights, and Ibsen, too, represented the bourgeois drama which he was interested in subverting and in replacing with some other dramatic form. Now, of course, to one who rejected the individual, the realistic or naturalistic play could not but become an impossible mode. Curiously enough, the Communist theoreticians of the theatre strongly supported realistic and naturalistic techniques in playwrighting, acting, and even stage design. (One must except Meyerhold, but he was liquidated by Stalin.) The Communists were for the Stanislavsky type of theatre, with its concentration on close analysis of individual motivation in a realistic setting. But Brecht, even when he became converted to Communism as a political doctrine, never yielded to the Communist theory of what theatre should be. The Communists of course did not believe in the individual or in moral experience any more than Brecht did, but they did not want to admit this publicly since they were interested in appealing to individuals and in justifying Com-

* See the preceding piece on Brecht.

munism morally. For them the theatre had value insofar as
it could make propaganda for their policies; for Brecht
the theatre could have value only insofar as it expressed
the convictions he felt deeply. He could not write realistic
plays about individuals, treating their moral conflicts seriously, since he thought the individual a phantom, and hence
the dramatization of moral sufferings would have to be
comical rather than serious. Certainly the Ibsen type of
drama was an impossibility for him, and he knew this from
the start.

It is very interesting, too, that he felt strongly opposed
to any form of tragedy. Much of what he has written on
this topic is uninteresting, since his objections to tragedy
are generally framed in the context of an attack on what
he terms the Aristotelian play, and by way of defending
a kind of rambling, loose-knit, reviewlike type of play,
favored early in the thirties by Piscator and which both
Brecht and Piscator designated by the term "epic theatre."
It is to be noted, though, that at the time Brecht opposed
his own epic theatre to Aristotelian theatre, he was much
more interested in the propaganda content of his plays than
later on in his most creative period, when he admitted that
the fundamental purpose of theatre had to be art and di-
version rather than propaganda or edification. In any case,
the term "epic theatre" is not a very clear one and has
little value in the way of explaining the great plays Brecht
came to write finally.

But obviously one could not write tragedy if one did not
believe in the importance of moral suffering. Thus Brecht
was opposed both to the mode of psychological realism,
a mode still fashionable in this country, and to the violent
fillip given that mode by Ibsen, who had imposed a necessitarian structure on his realistic plays, a structure taken
from Greek tragedy.

Actually, Brecht was not spontaneously opposed to implacable values, and in fact, had a kind of yearning for
them. His play *The Measures Taken,* analyzed previously,
may even be described as an experiment in submitting to
implacable values. It is the one play of his, too, which comes
close to tragedy. What prevents it from being deeply tragic,
though, is that the victim in the play, destroyed because he

is an individual, is only that abstractly, by definition. We never feel his individuality, and the recital of his death is not moving. But, in any case, the Communist Party, in its disapproval of *The Measures Taken,* indicated that it did not want Communist values to be expressed in absolute terms.

II

I have defined metatheatre as resting on two basic postulates: (1) the world is a stage and (2) life is a dream. Now I am not going to assert that Brecht entertained either of these postulates as truths to be demonstrated by his works. What I do claim is that Brecht, by having rejected the significance of the individual and of moral experience, had to rely on these concepts to give his plays form.

Let us look first at the proposition "the world is a stage." If one does not believe that individuals are real or their sufferings of any great moment, then do not all human actions, reactions, and expressions of feeling immediately seem theatrical? Now what was Brecht's most characteristic theatrical device? It was his deliberate insistence that feelings be played by his actors as if they were acted and not directly felt. One of his favorite devices was to ask his actors to act out a feeling as if they were telling of how some other person felt. Surely this is the furthest possible extreme from the kind of psychological realism we get regularly on the American stage, based very often on the notion that the most infantile and absurd expressions of feeling of so-called individuals are of the very greatest importance. Whether, then, Brecht believed the world to be a stage or not, his plays, his concepts of acting and stage design, were all calculated to produce that effect. The reality in his plays is that of theatre and not that of life, except as the latter happens to become theatrical. Ronald Gray says that Brecht's technical innovations were almost always in the direction of making the action on the stage not believable but "strange."

The other proposition of metatheatre is more difficult to ascribe to Brecht than the first. Could this hardheaded, practical-minded man have believed that life is a dream?

Again I do not think he would have consciously asserted
any such thing. But if one does not see any inner necessity
in the lives of people, will not their lives appear dreamlike? Brecht was so far from finding inner necessity in the
lives of persons that in *A Man's a Man* he even dramatized
the foisting by others of a new identity on his main character. I think in the main it is by the fact that they are
capable of feeling pain that others proclaim they are real to
us. And by sympathizing with their feelings we in fact
maintain their reality. Cool, dispassionate thinking of
the sort Brecht always advocated, and claimed he wanted
to induce in his spectators, is precisely the kind of thinking
that can never assert the reality of any person not oneself.
Life, in a way, had to be a dream for Brecht, given his
extreme devaluation of individual feelings.

Now the type of play Brecht wrote—it is the same type
of play that Shaw and Pirandello developed and is now
being done by Beckett and Genet—implies the notion
that life is a dream, and that the spectator will either form
this notion or feel its suggestiveness as a result of the play's
effect. Perhaps Brecht did not want this to happen, and I
think it correct to say he did not want this to happen because of his political views. Hence his idea of interfering
with, interrupting, restraining the response of the spectator.
Note that no writer of tragedy ever did or could be conceived as doing what Brecht set himself to do. For the
effect of tragedy is to induce in the spectator an almost
overwhelming sense of reality. You cannot call a spectator
back to reality from a tragic moment, for that moment, if
truly realized by the dramatist, is a concentrate of reality
beyond anything that might be felt in life, and certainly
beyond any sense of things that one might feel when stimulated to exercise one's "critical" powers. Certainly Brecht's
idea of recalling the spectator back from involvement would
be a contradictory one had Brecht been trying to write
tragedy or realism; it is not contradictory, considering that
what he actually wrote was metatheatre.

Here we may compare Brecht with Shaw, whose political
and social views were not dissimilar to those of the German
dramatist. Unquestionably Shaw used the theatre as a plat-
form for criticizing society, and he would have furiously

protested against our ascribing to him any such notion as
that life is a dream. But when we look at some of his finest
works this is what they say. Take such a masterpiece as
Pygmalion, for example. Here we have the complete trans-
formation of a vulgar, dirty, and illiterate girl into a dazzling
lady, brought about by cleansing her, dressing her, and
altering her diction. The play is incidentally a Cinderella
story. And let us consider *Don Juan in Hell*. This is a
thoroughgoing metaplay. Each character in it comes directly
from the stage and the opera. Each one of them has behind
him Tirso de Molina, Molière, and Mozart. The place is
hell, which, according to Shaw, is a place of illusion.
Heaven is for serious-minded people like Rembrandt or
Nietzsche, whom we never see and know of only through
their admirer Don Juan, who finally decides at the play's
close to be as serious as his heroes and to join them in
heaven. This decision may be taken to stand for Shaw's
personal feeling that life ought not be regarded as a dream
and that one should not take it as such. But the play he
wrote, the place he was interested in describing, was hell,
namely, according to his own view, the place of illusion.
Comparing Shaw's *Don Juan* with Brecht, one might say
that the German dramatist went one step further. Don
Juan merely announces he will go to heaven; Brecht assumed he was already there, that is, in the heaven of the
Communist movement. However, his plays, since capitalism
still existed, could take place only in hell and hence would
have to share hell's characteristics. But from his strategic
seat in the Communist heaven, the German playwright
could call out from time to time, interrupt and divert attention from the action of his own productions. Such, I
think, might be the explanation of Brecht's famous theory
of "alienating" the spectator.

Tragedy—or Metatheatre?

THE GREATEST PLAYWRIGHT in the nineteenth century was,
no doubt, influenced by Goethe's *Faust* in writing his own

piece of metatheatre, *Peer Gynt*. Here again we have a drama of philosophical depth expressed in fantasy, mixing comedy and satire. And again we have a self-referring character, Peer Gynt, a kind of milder, more mediocre, and more bourgeois Faust. Shaw thought Ibsen's play the greatest comedy ever written; Shaw, however, was wrong in calling it a comedy; Ibsen's gift for comedy was not marked. But in *Peer Gynt* the seriousness of the great Norwegian, shining through all of his plays, becomes exceptionally subtle, evocative, and delicate.

Ibsen did not later continue to work with the form he handled so masterfully in *Peer Gynt*. He was attracted on the one hand by the new realistic vision of life already expressed in the European novel, and on the other by the necessitarian structure of fated events which he found in Greek tragedy. And he devoted his genius, for much of his life, to unifying his critical and highly realistic observations of middle-class life in Norway with a dramatic form derived from Sophocles.

There was a great perception in this effort of Ibsen's. He must have realized that no form of drama gives such a compelling effect of the real as does the form of tragedy. Why not utilize that form along with direct observation of people and places? Why not combine the realist's critical attitude of mind with the tragic poet's feeling for the ultimately real in action, and thus produce the most overpowering illusion of reality ever achieved by any dramatist? Such must have been Ibsen's hope in writing *Ghosts, Hedda Gabler, The Wild Duck, Rosmersholm,* and *The Master Builder*.

So stated, Ibsen's objective seems a valid one. It always seems a valid hope to combine widely separate modes of thinking into a new pattern. Yet the strength of the human mind is not expressed in marriages of convenience, but, I think, as Ibsen might have learned from Kierkegaard, in the resolute confrontation of a real "either, or." I believe that it is in the light provided by the burning of its own bridges that the mind can best see. When Pizarro burned his own ships, he had all Peru at his mercy.

What did Ibsen achieve in the realistic "tragedies" of his most productive period? He never convinces us of the

necessity for the fate of Oswald in *Ghosts*, of Hedda
Gabler in his play about her, of Hedvig in *The Wild Duck*,
of Solness in *The Master Builder*, of Rosmer and Rebecca
West in *Rosmersholm*. His critically observed characters
are alive, and today his plays still live. But the "fatality"
suggested in his dramas remains suggested, and does not
convince us finally. Take *Ghosts*. The play would be just
as moving and much truer to its real subject, the rigidity
of Norwegian middle-class society, if Oswald did not have
hereditary syphilis and were simply "disturbed"—he is that
anyway—as a result of his separation from parents whose
marriage was unsatisfactory.

There is an artificial imposition of fate on his characters,
which today makes us feel some of Ibsen's greatest works
are clumsy and contrived—often unreal. In a certain sense,
the truth of Ibsen is in Chekhov, who, powerfully influenced by Tolstoy's insistence on utter truthfulness, deliberately softened the oppositions in his plays, toned down
their climaxes, broke up the structure of the "well-made
play," of which Ibsen was so proud, and eliminated altogether any suggestion that what happened to his characters
happened because of fate. Interestingly enough, Chekhov
was able to do all this and yet produce plays which have
some dynamism because of an accidental fact of history:
the characters he presents are derived from the Russian
intelligentsia, which European history, long before Chekhov
became a dramatist, had already placed on the stage.

Thus Chekhov could produce a kind of metatheatre
while remaining genuinely realistic. The characters he described were already theatrical. Social forces had doomed
the Russian intelligentsia to extinction; their consciousness
of this, though, was what interested Chekhov, not the fate-
fulness of their situation. And insofar as Chekhov ever
yields to the sense of fatality—as he does in *The Cherry
Orchard*—instead of magnifying it or making it more
drastic, his whole effort is to render it delicately. He
understood, no doubt, that there was no such thing as fate,
even in the historical sense of that term, without the willing
collaboration of men.

There is another point I want to make about Ibsen's
peculiar effort and the results of that effort on subsequent

dramatists. There is something else about tragedy which is interesting besides the fact that it thrusts one against the ultimately real: in a true tragedy one is beyond thought. Thus the writer of a tragedy does not have to express ideas. He only has to have, as the phrase goes—I do not think it a good one—"a tragic view of life." Actually, Ibsen, supposedly an intellectual playwright, was strikingly lacking in ideas. When in *Rosmersholm* Rosmer speaks of carrying out "the new ideas" one never knows what he has in mind. *The Wild Duck* becomes absurd insofar as Gregers Werle has no genuinely intellectual motive for making the revelation he makes to Hjalmar Ekdal, which results in the painful suicide of Hedvig. In *Ghosts,* Ibsen makes Mrs. Alving too easily superior to Pastor Manders for any real criticism of the Protestant clergy to emerge in that play. When Kierkegaard attacked the Protestant church, he attacked the greatest Protestant pastors of Denmark; Ibsen's Pastor Manders is a plain fool. How could the Protestant church be made ridiculous by the exhibition of Manders' mainly personal folly?

If the truth of Ibsen is in Chekhov, Ibsen's false tragedy is to be found particularly in the American theatre, whose outstanding playwrights so far, Eugene O'Neill, Tennessee Williams, and Arthur Miller, are all continuers and imitators of Ibsen. Here (for once) I agree with Mary McCarthy, who has pointed up the dependence of the realistic school of American playwrights on the work of the great Norwegian. Miss McCarthy is quite wrong, however, in saying that all realistic plays are badly written. O'Neill and Tennessee Williams, at least, are excellent writers; Ibsen was a great writer and, as Eliot said, actually made prose do what before him only the verse form could.

What *is* true of O'Neill, Tennessee Williams, and Arthur Miller, though, is that all of them were attracted to Ibsen's form because it suggests the possibility of a serious play without the dramatist's having any need to think—except dramatically. Like Ibsen, and thanks to him, these playwrights have accomplished what they have without the need for ideas.

If Shaw, who admired Ibsen so greatly, was never an imitator of Ibsen, this was because Shaw had a gift for comedy, which Ibsen lacked, and also because Shaw had an interest in expressing ideas. There is an intellectual structure in most of Shaw's important plays which we do not find in Ibsen at all. Moreover, in addition to his irrepressible and beneficent humor, the Irish playwright had a feeling for philosophical drama. Thus I account for his having written works of metatheatre without having thought seriously of going beyond the form of comedy. The *Don Juan in Hell* episode (a complete play in itself), *Pygmalion*, and *Saint Joan* are not comedies, but metaplays.

When Shaw saw a performance of Pirandello's *Six Characters in Search of an Author*, he is said to have remarked: "This playwright is greater than I am." If true, the story would indicate that Shaw was sensitive to a dramatic form irrelevant to his own social and moral purposes. For the effect of Pirandello's *Six Characters in Search of an Author* is not at all upon the critical reason, but almost entirely on the metaphysical imagination. In fact, the Italian dramatist is lacking in moral interest: his dramaturgy counts only when he is excited by the metaphysical side of a conflict.

One might say that Pirandello was the epistemologist of metatheatre, not its ontologist. Pirandello is always interesting when he explores dramatically our inability to distinguish between illusion and reality; he was not prepared to assert, though, that the unreal *is*. Illusion, for Pirandello, was that which defines the limits of human subjectivity. But for the contemporary playwright, Jean Genet, illusion is something objective, something splendid, too, not an error. Thus in *The Balcony*, the characters are most real when dressed up for their peculiar roles. In *The Blacks*, the Negroes are presented not as perhaps Negroes feel themselves to be, but as they see themselves reflected in the mirror of the white race.

The logician of metatheatre was Bertolt Brecht. He took care to order not only his plays but also their décor and the style of acting he needed for them. He introduced an antinaturalistic logic into acting and stage design as well as into his own dramatic construction. His characters are his puppets, to be sure, but he insists on the fact that they are puppets, does not try to pass them off as real people, and delights in exhibiting their mechanisms. The cynicism

which modern dictators have shown toward real people
was in Brecht; he showed it toward his own characters.
Never could he have succeeded in doing so had he relied
on a realistic or naturalistic form of drama. What led him
to metatheatre? Certainly it was not reflection on past art,
nor was it some deep intuition of the importance of consciousness. But he did come to metatheatre; and having
come to it, he was more thorough about it than any other
playwright of his time.

So there are two trends in contemporary drama, one
going back to the Shaw of *Don Juan in Hell* and *Saint Joan,*
to Ibsen's *Peter Gynt,* and still further back to Shakespeare
and Calderón; the other springing from the realistic period
of Ibsen's so-called tragedies. This second trend does not go,
and cannot go, further back than Ibsen's works, for authentic tragedy, which can give a stronger feeling of reality than
"realism," implies an acceptance of values which contemporary writers are unlikely to hold. I shall not say that tragedy is impossible, or, as George Steiner has suggested, dead.
If Shakespeare, with his skepticism, could write even one
tragedy, there is no reason at all to assert that the form
is impossible to any modern dramatist, whatever his cast
of mind. A dramatist may appear to whom the Furies are
real—and I do not mean just symbolically real—and still
uncompromising in their demands for blood vengeance, as
they were before Aeschylus pacified them in the third part
of his *Oresteia.** Hegel thought that after *Hamlet,* all modern tragedies would be tragedies of the intellectual. I think
he should have said tragedy would be replaced by metatheatre.

* Are not the witches in *Macbeth* something like the Furies of
the *Oresteia,* but more morally ambiguous, more symbolical,
more literary, if you please, than the terrible figures in Aeschylus' work? Also, did not Shakespeare, to find them, have to
plunge into a darker and more superstitious past, whereas
Aeschylus was able to go with his Furies into the clear light of
Athenean society? Certainly, the pacification of the Furies in the
Oresteia made problematic the future of tragedy as an art form.
Modern dramatists, trying to restore that form, have been forced
to seek it among primitives: the Irish peasantry (Synge), the
Spanish peasants (Lorca), half-mad sinners of the sixteenth
century (Ghelderode), and, in America, culturally deprived
characters like the protagonists of *Death of a Salesman* and
A View from the Bridge.

To summarize the values and disvalues of tragedy and metatheatre:

Tragedy gives by far the stronger sense of the reality of the world. Metatheatre gives by far the stronger sense that the world is a projection of human consciousness.

Tragedy glorifies the structure of the world, which it supposedly reflects in its own form. Metatheatre glorifies the unwillingness of the imagination to regard any image of the world as ultimate.

Tragedy makes human existence more vivid by showing its vulnerability to fate. Metatheatre makes human existence more dreamlike by showing that fate can be overcome.

Tragedy tries to mediate between the world and man. Tragedy wants to be on both sides. Metatheatre assumes there is no world except that created by human striving, human imagination.

Tragedy cannot operate without the assumption of an ultimate order. For metatheatre, order is something continually improvised by men.

There is no such thing as humanistic tragedy. There is no such thing as religious metatheatre. George Lukacs has said that the principal spectator of tragedy is God. I cannot imagine God present at a play of Shaw, Pirandello, or Genet. I cannot imagine Godot enjoying *Waiting for Godot*.

Tragedy, from the point of view of metatheatre, is our dream of the real. Metatheatre, from the point of view of tragedy, is as real as are our dreams.

Nicolai Hartmann distinguishes the "depth of succession" from the "breadth of simultaneity." The first is the province of tragedy. The second belongs to metatheatre.

Tragedy transcends optimism and pessimism, taking us beyond both these attitudes. Metatheatre makes us forget the opposition between optimism and pessimism by forcing us to wonder.

Shall we not stop lamenting the "death" of tragedy and value justly the dramatic form which Western civilization—and that civilization only—has been able to create and to refine?

RELEVANCIES

Bad by North and South

NORTH: I've been sent a verse play to review—O, I'll review it. But don't people know that I'm opposed to plays in verse? I've said it often enough. From Djuna Barnes's *The Antiphon* I've gotten further arguments to back up my prejudice. I'm more against the whole enterprise of so-called "poetic drama" than ever.

SOUTH: I have a bad verse play to review, too, Archibald MacLeish's *J.B.* But I'm not opposed to verse plays in general, as you are. After all, even if both of these works are as bad as we think, that doesn't mean the form as such is to be condemned. What if someone writes a good verse play?

NORTH: Most unlikely.

SOUTH: What about *Murder in the Cathedral*?

NORTH: That was not bad, to be sure. Very good, in fact. It's about the best thing we have in the genre. Nevertheless, I don't consider it an important play, and as Edmund Wilson noted, the one really good dramatic scene in it, is in prose. . . .

SOUTH: You told me you're against verse drama, but not why.

NORTH: *The Antiphon* is a perfect example of what is wrong with this kind of play. You get the impression that each character is trying to make a poem of his or her feelings; no one is swept into speech by action or emotion. Now who wants to go to the theatre to watch people writing poetry? In this activity, there is indeed labor and pain, but not the kind of labor or pain we can enjoy—unless the result is a poem we ourselves produce.

SOUTH: But do not even Shakespeare's characters sometimes give the impression that they are writing poems?

NORTH: They do, at times, and at such times, the less Shakespearean they.

SOUTH: I was thinking of Othello's

> It is the cause, It is the cause, my soul:
> Let me not name it to you, O chaste stars!
> It is the cause. Yet I'll not shed her blood . . .

NORTH: Let's take these lines. There is, of course, an element of "poetry writing" in them, at least in the first two lines, but in the third Othello quickly comes to the point when he says

> Yet I'll not shed her blood . . .

which directly relates him to the act before him. However, all references to the verse plays of the Elizabethans—and of Shakespeare in particular—when applied to the problem of the modern verse play, are very misleading. Poetical expression, I take it, was more spontaneous under the Elizabeth of those days, than of ours. It was, if you like, prereflective; nowadays, it is postreflective. The last person you would expect to express himself—nowadays, that is—with poetic eloquence, would be a simple person involved in a serious action. The person most likely to express himself in life with poetic eloquence would be someone who had given thought to the problems of poetry. Nowadays, it takes *time* to write a poem, a lot of time to write a *modern* poem, and what we want on the stage, is the direct, immediate expression of feeling. You know something? I mean I want to tell you something you may not know: I would be interested in reading a verse play that was written overnight, as it is claimed that some of Lope de Vega's plays were. But I think the thing is impossible. I am sure the play I just read by Djuna Barnes must have taken years to compose. One result is that the characters scarcely talk to each other. Each one is intent on subtilizing and distilling his own thought and feeling into a verse expression adequate to the author's norms of rhetoric, and these are not at all dramatic norms. The result: there is no dialogue in any proper sense of the term in this play, and the words spoken by any one character have scarcely any effect on the others. It is as if the real action lay in the production of words, poetic words, and as if each character was too exhausted by this effort to listen to what the others have to say.

SOUTH: Your judgment of Djuna Barnes's *The Antiphon* may be correct, but I think the play I have to review, MacLeish's *J.B.*, is worse, though in exactly the opposite way. Take the title, for instance. *J.B.* is, of course, short for Job. Now Job is short, and wonderfully so, as short as a cry, or a lifetime. Why abbreviate the name that sums up all abridgments and abbreviations? To bring Job up to date. But why bring Job up to date when there is nothing antiquated about him? Just as the name, which is so wonderful, is diminished poetically by the initials J. B., even so the story is banalized by being consciously placed in a modern setting. What makes MacLeish's play so objectionable is the author's effort to make it a real theatrical work with gags, punch lines, fast dialogue. We get all the dramaturgical tricks that are required by Broadway audiences; but every once in a while, the author sneaks in here and there a great line from the old book. Now I am not against Mr. MacLeish's trying to write a verse play, since no matter what you say, I remain unconvinced that the form, as such, is impossible. What I find obnoxious is MacLeish's utter lack of poetic inspiration, and his acceptance of cheap dramatic standards in retelling one of the greatest stories of our literature.

NORTH: I think I'm against cheap dramatic standards as much as you are.

SOUTH: What I am driving at is that the great affliction of drama is not, as you seem to think, that people are trying to write plays in verse. I'm inclined to think that type of effort a very commendable one, no matter how great the difficulty is. What I can't stand about MacLeish is his utter thoughtlessness. He has no point of view toward the story of Job that could justify his retelling it. Here is what I mean: a famous modern philosopher has said that the greatest tribute to being is for someone to desire not to be. The greatest tributes to being in literature, then, would be Job's curse of the day on which he was born, the choruses in Oedipus, and Hamlet's famous soliloquy. These would be the moments when being really *was;* they happen to be the greatest moments in our dramatic literature. Now from this point of view, we could understand why God preferred Job's curse of his own birth to the practical advice of Job's friends; also, why in response to Job's curse, God asserts the mere fact that He is. Now I'm not saying that a good drama about Job could be written from such a point of view, interesting though the view is. I'm trying to suggest something else; all the modern mind can add to the old story is reflection; now reflection is not the basis for a dramatic work. On the other hand, why take up a story of this kind if one has no significant thoughts about it? I do think drama is only possible where the dramatist's thought is involved, and where that thought is a direct, immediate, intuitively perceived sense of the meaning of some action.

NORTH: Now you're coming around to my point of view, that poetry is impossible in drama when it is postreflective. You're going even further, saying that the dramatist's thought should be prereflective; and I'm inclined to agree with you about that, too. Unless the dramatist relied on some form which could reconcile the dramatic and the reflective. . . . But let me give you an example of the kind of speeches we get in Djuna Barnes's *The Antiphon:*

> That was the day that story-book Augusta
> Feather-headed, fairy-tale Augusta
> In her mind's wild latitude laid out
> And armed such battlefield, tilt patch and list
> As out-geared Mars. My maximed mind
> Out-maximed circus Maximus.
> I hung the bright shields up, I spun the drill,
> Clubbed the spears and standards, ax and mace.
> I teased the olive, and all budding things
> Into the loop that wheels a victor's head
> And for his blood their own bright berries drop

Now I won't make the obvious point that no human being would ever talk like that. What I will say is that it would be impossible for even the most intelligent audience to decipher the meaning of these lines when hearing them spoken on the stage. But I want to make a still further point, and thus bring out the difference between a stage work and a piece of writing which looks like a play yet really isn't one. Now then, suppose the audience for Miss Barnes's *The Antiphon* could be cajoled into studying her play before seeing it: what would be their reward? They could not have an immediate contact with the play until after they had studied it—which means they could never have an immediate contact with it. They would have to know the play by heart to hear it—that is, to see it—for the first time! Let me put the matter differently. A really good dramatic work should reveal itself most essentially when produced. I never really understood the Antigone, not of Anouilh, but of Sophocles, until I saw it done on the stage by the Comédie Française. But it is quite clear that no light could be thrown on Miss Barnes's play by any production of it. I have read it through twice, and I am still not sure I have gotten the story in its dramatic details. . . .

SOUTH: Can you be so sure it's bad if you don't know what it's about?

NORTH: Oh, I know what it's about. Or, to be precise, I know what it means, rather than exactly what happens in it. And this, I think, is the play's fault, not mine. . . . *The Antiphon* is an Electra play. The action takes place in a contemporary setting—the time is 1939—and there is no supernatural machinery, which, from my point of view, would be all to the good, if there were only some other kind of machinery—that is, plot—to get the action going. But there is scarcely any action, the play being the end and term of what happened before offstage. Here, too, we have a modernization of an old myth, but with much more justification, apparently, than in the case of MacLeish's handling of the Job story. Miss Barnes *does* have a reason for modernizing, personalizing her Electra figure, for in *The Antiphon,* the daughter represents to the mother the full horror of what has happened to her at the hands of the father, as well as representing all the humiliations women have suffered at the hands of men. Miss Barnes's Electra, parodying the Ghost's "Hamlet, remember me!" in *Hamlet,* says to her mother, "Woman, remember you." But the mother does not have the strength for this, and the play ends with her murder of her daughter. I should add that there are several male characters, including an Orestes and a Pedagogue, all with good English names, of course. And the general theme of the play is rather strong: the horror of what men do to women in making them mothers, and women to men in giving birth to them.

SOUTH: Now that sounds interesting!

NORTH: I don't deny a certain distinction in the writing. But I am judging *The Antiphon* as a play—I don't know if there are any categories for judging a closet-drama. A play has to be capable of being presented on the stage, as even Beddoes' *Death's Jest Book* could be, I believe. Now *The Antiphon* is simply unplayable. I note that on the book jacket Edwin Muir is quoted as saying it would be a "disaster" if this work were not known. The disaster of this work, I should say, is that it cannot be known. For it *cannot*

make itself known on the stage as its form requires it to do.
And how hard it is to read! I sat up all night over it, and
would never have kept on reading if I didn't have my review
to write.

SOUTH: I'm going to suggest that nobody read MacLeish's
J.B. or go to see it either, yet I read it quickly enough, in
about half an hour to be exact, and from it turned to the
Book of Job which took me all night.

NORTH: In any case, you see what modern verse plays are
like.

SOUTH: I still don't see why it should be impossible to
write a good one.

NORTH: I would not say that a good verse play is impossible to achieve. What I think is that such an accomplish-
ment is unlikely, and that what is unlikely is hardly a proper
object of a sensible man's activity. Now a good dramatist
must be fundamentally sensible.

SOUTH: Don't you think T.S. Eliot is?

NORTH: Unquestionably. But just look at his plays. He
has been writing prose plays disguised as verse ever since
Family Reunion. Since that work, which he himself admits
was a failure, he has devoted himself to writing a kind of
nonpoetic verse play. The results, if we are to judge by *The
Confidential Clerk* and *The Cocktail Party* are works which
are fundamentally prosaic—much more so than Chekhov's
plays in prose, for instance. Perhaps Mr. Eliot has to write
plays in the way he does since his whole sensibility had already been formed on the basis of verse when he turned to
the theatre. In that case he is a sport, an accident, a chance
event in the theatre. . . .

SOUTH: But *The Confidential Clerk* and *The Cocktail
Party* are in verse of a sort and they are good plays.

NORTH: Oh, I don't deny that. What I deny is that Eliot
has succeeded in what is the *main* task of a dramatist, which
is to produce a new dramatic system. Ibsen did that, and
Strindberg, and Shaw, Pirandello, and even Giraudoux.
Eliot did not, though he did create a poetic system before
he turned his hand to writing plays. Now my contention is
that no play can be truly poetic if it does not express the
discovery of a new dramatic system. Thus we get the paradox that all the playwrights I mentioned wrote dramas fundamentally more poetic than Mr. Eliot's, though none of

them, except for Ibsen in his early phase, wrote plays in verse. Perhaps I can now formulate more clearly what seems to me the almost insuperable difficulty of the verse play in our time. In the past, the creators of new dramatic systems made their discoveries *in verse,* since verse was the accepted medium. It is almost inconceivable that this type of discovery could be made today in verse, for the creation of an adequate verse for stage purposes would exhaust the invention of even the most gifted poet. Mr. Eliot's career in the theatre should be a warning that what we are going to get from the effort to bring poetry to the theatre will probably not be a revitalization of the theatrical art, but a compromised, flat, and diluted poetry, which can scarcely uplift us either on or off the stage. Have I convinced you?

SOUTH: My problem is to convince my readers that I am right about MacLeish's *J.B.*

NORTH: And I must convince mine that Djuna Barnes's *The Antiphon* is no worse than they should have expected.

Not Everyone Is in the Fix

YOU ARE NOT where you wanted to be, nor will you get what you expected. But do you want to go somewhere else? Where? Not easy to say, but it's not easy to stay where you are, either. You will stay too, unless you are like the reviewers for the dailies, who damned this play* almost to a man. Why will you stay? Not in any great hope of pleasure, but as you stay in a dentist's office, motivated by an aching tooth. If you had come to be relieved of your boredom, then you will not be satisfied. You will not be relieved. You will be even more bored than you were when you first came in. More bored and more amenable to further boredom, a state in which there is a certain fascination. You are bored stiff by the junkies on the stage; they are bored stiff too, with each other and with themselves. They are waiting for a "flash." What are you waiting for? They know what they want. You might decide of course that you know you don't

* *The Connection,* by Jack Gelber, first presented at the Living Theatre in New York City.

want to wait with them. But for some reason you do wait,
until their chance for a "flash" comes. And while you wait
as they wait, certainly not for God and not even for Godot,
you lose your perspective, that is, assuming you had one; in
this there is a definite pleasure. The fact of the matter is
you don't know what you are doing or why you go anywhere. Probably that is why you have come to see *The
Connection*. And on the stage there are people, recogniza-
bly real, who are as disoriented as you are, but know that
they want something, or at least need something. They are
waiting for "horse," that is to say, heroin; it will be brought
to them by a Negro appropriately named Cowboy. Shall
"horse" take them somewhere, and you along with them?
Can you jump on after them and gallop out of your dull
time into some undrugged eternity? This is not to happen.
They get their dose of heroin but I think you will get no
charge out of their "flash." After the waiting there is little
release, the same dissatisfaction. These people certainly take
no special attitudes; they're immersed in ordinary life, just
as you are. No one is particularly bad, nobody notably good.
Anyway, moral postures are hardly taken, and clearly do
not count. If there is any hero, it is Cowboy, who gets the
stuff, takes the risks involved in getting it, administers it to
the others, and behaves generally like the doctor which his
white uniform makes us feel he is. Does he take the stuff
himself? Probably. But certainly there must be a greater
thrill for him in getting hold of it. Also, he is master of the
situation; he alone determines the quantity of each dose,
how much each junkie can take, what amount might be
fatal. Is there anyone who can ride "horse"? If anyone, that
one is Cowboy. Yet we never see him take the stuff, and in
this fact I see the only concession to conventional morality
made by the talented young playwright, Jack Gelber.

Dull the place is, dismal the prospects, cretins the people,
and yet you don't have a desire to go home. Certainly the
music keeps you. The musicians, stacked up like instruments
for most of the time, come alive once or twice or maybe
three times, and improvise brilliantly, beautifully; this is
music such as one seldom hears. However, the music is
merely an interruption of the waiting; it serves better, I will
grant, than a movie would between the time you get to a
station and the time your train is supposed to leave. After

all, the musicians are also in the fix. They too are waiting
for "horse." And when they get "horse," they, at least, do
something: they play, and marvelously. "Horse" really takes
them somewhere, and us also. But not for long and not far
enough. We come back.

And now a question is forced on us—it was insinuated
all along—but we only come to recognize it after a while.
The question is: What do we want, we who are not junkies,
if we are not? Don't we too want a "flash" of one kind or
other? A "horse" of some sort, a charge, if you please, a
sharp sensation, a quick connection? Does any of us want
something more than that? The "flash" may be a new girl, a
new thought, a new job, a new compliment; what is the
difference between these and the connection the people we
watch are waiting for? And you will wonder: Am I different
from these junkies? Do I aim at more than a few sensations,
and if I think I do, isn't this because I have shored up my
pride and health against ruin with a number of platitudes?
Can you answer these questions? If you can, you'll be able
to get up and leave the play at its most exciting moment,
which, by the way, is not terribly exciting. But if you cannot
answer these questions (and how many can?) then you will
have to stay to the very end, which is long in coming, and
scarcely distinguishable from the beginning. *The Connection* is a moral trap; but nowadays people like to get caught.
Why not?

What adds to the play's power is that the characters are
so like other people, though in such a different situation
from most people. The junkies of *The Connection* are no
"invalids of happiness." They are not people who have paid
a great price for a great joy; if they were, they would be on
a higher level than their audience; they would have a right
to be on the stage. They don't have that right, in fact, except
that Jack Gelber was cunning enough to put them there.
There ensconced, they dominate, mainly by being so similar
to the people watching them, which means also to you.

How many plays ask a real question as this one does?
The answer is evident, and makes of *The Connection* something outstanding. I must add, too, that it is brilliantly directed and admirably played. It lacks incident, but why
should there be any in such a work? I must add, too, that
there are some Pirandellian details—I mean the playwright,

producer, and cameramen who intrude on the junkies to
harass and photograph them—which are not in keeping
with the general spirit of the work, and are, if the author
will forgive me, plain dumb. Certainly a better way to involve the audience with happenings on the stage would have
been for Cowboy to announce that anyone seated in the
theatre had a right to a shot of "horse." Actors could have
been stationed in the audience who would respond, and we
would have been fascinated by the possibility of being in
the fix too.

Heroin, I understand, does not induce beautiful dreams
as opium and hashish do; this is not a drug for aesthetes;
Baudelaire would not have favored it. Heroin is the drug
of hijackers and band players; a Faustian drug, then, one
which adds risk to risk, danger to danger, exhilaration to
action. Certainly this particular drug seems consonant with
the character of the times; it is not eccentric to take it while
taking hashish or opium would be. Curiously enough, if we
are normal people, not too odd, we have already opted for
heroin even if we never take it. For if we were to become
addicts, this would be our drug. Our lives turn toward it,
and away from the more "aesthetic" drugs. So still another
question is asked by the play: Why don't we too take
heroin? We are, in fact, connected with it.

Not that there is any propaganda in this work in favor of
addiction, for there is none of that. And thank God, there is
no moral cant either; no moralizing à la Broadway. Nobody
is shown on the stage in a state of torment because he would
like to give up taking heroin. The torment of these people,
and ours, too, insofar as we identify ourselves with them,
is that for the space of more than two hours there is abso-
lutely nothing else to take but heroin. Only that.

As the effect of heroin relates to action rather than to
contemplation, so the play's focus is on moral rather than
aesthetic values. Certainly there is little beauty on the
Living Theatre stage; no pleasure at all to the eye, little in
the language spoken. There is the thrilling music at times,
to be sure, but even this is disturbing. It too suggests the
drug which is to be or has been taken. Why go to see such
a play? Why expose oneself to the nagging question: what's
better than "horse"? Speak up.

I think it is the moral difficulty one feels in answering

that gives this play its fascination. But to be fascinated is to admit to being without goal or purpose, to be unable to justify one's undrugged and apparently directed actions. Fascination or pride, we prefer fascination.

So the play judges its spectators, and the latter's judgment of it scarcely counts, be it favorable or unfavorable. What does aesthetic judgment matter? What is really of import is surely not one's judgment of dramatic merits or demerits. What matters is what matters most: life itself, how you and I live it, with what aim, what resolve, what enjoyment. What but prudence would keep us from getting on the stage ourselves if Cowboy did indeed offer to minister to us too? There is the thing forbidden; but what is so bad about it? No effort has been made to make it seem alluring; the whole business of waiting for it, getting it, taking it, and getting that all-meaningful "flash" from it has been shown in as grim a way as the most conventional moralist could wish. No, there is nothing wonderful about taking heroin, not according to what I saw in *The Connection*. The disturbing thing, though, is the insinuation of the question: what else is wonderful?

For how many people, I wonder, is anything wonderful? If there are as many in that fix as I think, and if the play's effect is as salutary as I assume it to be, people everywhere should be urged to see it. I promise faithfully that whenever I see anyone in a state of moral disarray, spiritual collapse, worry about his goals, I shall send him to see *The Connection*. A play, of course, cannot provide one with a new spiritual state, but only sustain whatever spiritual state you have brought with you into the theatre. Anyone who finds his life boring will find *The Connection* less so. But this is not for people who know what to do with their time.

There are what have been called "high" experiences. These are limited in number, we can count them: love, friendship, heroic adventure, martyrdom (this is ambiguous, it is probably the lowest—not meaning by "lowest" basest— as well as the highest of experiences), the act of creation. Not much has been left out of this list, but it will be noted that for very few people are many of these so-called "high" experiences possible, particularly today, and they are becoming increasingly less so. In fact the widespread yearning for artistic creation on the part of so many people not gifted in that special way reflects something negative, not something positive. Namely, the absence of "high" experiences of another sort. But to come back to *The Connection,* is getting "high" a high experience? My judgment would be that it is not. But what is the view of the author? At one point in the play we have the following absurd and yet revealing incident: when the junkies are finally getting their shots of heroin and are being photographed by the cameramen, who are presumably to make a film about dope addiction, the writer of the script rushes onto the stage and begs for a shot, too. He, who can create something, needs the "flash" like the others. Who that cannot create doesn't need it?

A play is essentially a game but a game played with something sacred. A play is seldom made badly simply because the playwright doesn't know the game—dramaturgy is not as difficult an art as is generally thought, and most playwrights, even hacks, are able to pick up at least the elementary rules, occasionally even some of the finer points. What makes most plays bad is the fact that the playwright does not genuinely feel as sacred the particular value or experience which he pretends to so regard for the sake of his play's structure. For actually, the question of the sacredness of something is intimately linked to the very form of any play. I always notice in bad dramatic works the moment when the dramatist begins to pretend to have an enthusiasm for some value which his whole work belies. The falsely sacred—that is the bane of the theatre. Whatever be the faults of *The Connection,* it does not give us that. In this play something really is at stake: our estimation of our pleasures, their occasionalness and their worth, our estimate of our health too, for what good is it unless we can be enthusiastic about something else than merely retaining it? There is nothing delightful in *The Connection,* little poetry, and a degree of pain; but from the fact that we are shaken up, disturbed, and self-questioning when we leave the theatre, we know that we have seen a good show.

The Living Theatre

EVER SINCE Jack Gelber's *The Connection,* damned by the New York newspaper critics, stayed on the boards to win their praise, the Living Theatre, which staged the play, has gone from success to success. It is now a respected institution, not only in New York, but throughout Europe; even those who do not like it say: "After all—it's alive."

This season, the Living Theatre staged a new play by Gelber: *The Apple.* And the newspaper reviewers were much more respectful, though not completely enthusiastic. Should one be completely enthusiastic about *The Apple?* Or were the newspaper critics wrong once again, wrong this time for withholding their fire?

Now I found *The Apple* an authentically unbrilliant play with an authentically unbrilliant message. What it says is: Be an imbecile.

I was one of those who praised *The Connection,* but I remember wondering, after justifying my praise of it, what Jack Gelber's next play would be like. It is to be hoped that his third play will have some of the solidity and seriousness of his first. For *The Apple* is gimmicky from beginning to end. And its gimmicks are only mildly interesting. Though, to be fair, they are occasionally infused with a note of that "wretched lyricism" which Harold Clurman noted and admired—rightly—in *The Connection.*

To be sure, the dramatic concept which the Living Theatre specializes in is essentially a gimmicky one; this is not to say that the concept is either good or bad, but only that it is limited. Certainly there is a place in life and on the stage for gimmicks and gimmickyness. But why, it may be asked, should an institution calling itself the Living Theatre be gimmicky? And mainly that? My answer is: "living theatre" always was.

What, then, is meant by "living theatre"? To my mind, something not exactly new. On the contrary, something that occurs occasionally in most plays, and that has been singled out for special attention by Judith Malina, Julian Beck (the directors), Jack Gelber, and their fellows. For example, in a rather poor play of Sartre's, *Lucifer and the Lord,* written during the Korean war while MacArthur was still in command, Sartre made one of his characters, a bourgeois of the sixteenth century, say of a general: it would be best to remove him from his post, but can a civilian fire a general? This crack was a pure political gimmick, intended to excite the anti-American feelings of Parisians of that period. Unfortunately for Jean-Paul Sartre, by the time his play was produced Truman had removed MacArthur, and the crack fell flat.

There are cracks of this type in probably every Broadway play, some of them opportune, others too early or too late. But why should an institution of the theatre devote itself to this type of effect? My own view is that whatever is alive will have enough energy to think up some *raison d'être* or justification for itself; such justification, however, is unlikely to be that it is "living."

Let us go back several hundred years. Cervantes, who was a fair playwright before he became a great novelist, at some point in his career tried his hand at "living theatre" too. He wrote a number of plays which aimed at affecting the audience directly instead of at moving them through the force or beauty of the story he had to tell. Take *The Marvelous Pageant.* In this Cervantes work, two unscrupulous showmen put on a performance in a Spanish town. They explain beforehand to the Governor why their show is bound to be surefire:

On account of the marvelous things that appear and are shown in it, it came to be called the Marvelous Pageant. It was manufactured and compounded by the learned Foolfoorello . . . [in such a way] that no one can see the things that appear in it if he have in his ancestry a trace of Jewish blood, or if he be not begotten and procreated in lawful matrimony; and he who is touched with these two prevalent contagions, let him give up all hope of ever seeing the marvels . . . of my pageant.

The play, paid for in advance, is "put on" before the inhabitants of the town. When the audience is assembled, one of the showmen, Chanfalla, addresses them:

CHANFALLA: Attention, ladies and gentlemen, the performance is about to start!

O thou, whoever thou wert, who didst construct this pageant with such a marvelous artifice that it gained fame. . . . I conjure thee, I compel thee, I command thee, instantly and immediately to display to these gentlemen some of thy marvelous marvels. . . . Ah, now I see thou hast granted my petition since over there appears the figure of mighty Samson, embracing the columns of the temple to pull it down and take vengeance on his enemies. Hold, valiant knight! . . . Commit not such an offense, in order not to crush and pulverize so many and such noble folk. . . .

BENITO (the Mayor): Stop, confound you! Wouldn't that be great, that we came here to have a good time and ended up by being squashed!

CAPACHO (Notary): Do you see him, Castrado?

JUAN (Alderman): Of course I see him! Are my eyes in the back of my head?

THE GOVERNOR (aside): This *is* a miraculous business! I don't see any Samson, any more than I see the Grand Turk; yet I consider myself a legitimate child and of a good old Christian family.

After Samson, the showmen "materialize" water from the source of the Jordan; blue, white, and speckled mice descended directly from the two in Noah's ark, a wild bull, lions, bears, and finally Salome, dancing. Members of the audience are then asked to dance with Salome, and the nephew of the Mayor obliges. The play terminates when the Quartermaster arrives. Not having heard the showman's speech at the beginning of the performance, he reacts naturally. When he sees the nephew of the Mayor dancing without a partner and the audience entranced by the wonderful couple, he concludes that everyone has gone mad. Because he does not see what the others "see," they call him "Jew" and "bastard' and he goes after everyone on the stage— actors and audience—with drawn sword.

This play of Cervantes charms at once, but what is the point of it? For one thing, it presents an audience on the stage, and the audience watching this audience is provided with some glimpse of itself: it is enabled to see itself seeing. Then, a real event is produced by the putting on of a false show, for the Quartermaster is not a spectator cozened into performing, nor is he a performer; he performs all the same, but his rage and exasperation are unfeigned. A real person puts an end to a show. But certainly Cervantes' chief aim was to amuse, by frightening, the real audience watching the false show. No one in the audience on the stage could get up and walk out for fear of being called "Jew" or "bastard," serious terms, these, in the Spain of Cervantes. But the real audience, watching that audience, could not but have had the same fear; this fear Cervantes manipulates marvelously. Here we have "living theatre" at its best.

The Apple is "living theatre" too, but not nearly so good. At the beginning of the play one of the actors, a Negro, threatens the audience:

You're going to witness and may be part of some destructive scenes. That might take over your mind and make you forget just how warm your body is. . . . This is no joking matter. We are going to eat up the set, the audience, and nibble a little on ourselves. . . .

Nothing of the sort takes place. But the audience of *The Apple* is supposed to fear for a moment that it is unsafe to be in the Living Theatre. Other ways of involving the audience directly are tried out. For instance, the Negro sells coffee to people in the front rows; the voices of the actors are sometimes heard from the rear through loudspeakers. Still one doesn't see how the activity on the stage could reach any real fear, or hope, or despair. For there is nothing in the effort of the production to get directly to the audience comparable to Cervantes' insinuation that anyone who walked out on his *Marvelous Pageant* might be a bastard or a Jew. Perhaps though, people enjoy *The Apple* with some fear: if they admitted to not enjoying it, they might be called squares.

Toward the end of the second act, the audience is addressed directly:

Come over to our side. You're not doing anything important. What do you do all day? Read the papers? You have a job! And you vote! You really make up your own mind? You don't know who you are until you're dead. Wouldn't you like to know? Life is so apathetic! Everything in your life changes from day to day. . . . Isn't it confusing and then just boring? Life is such a bore! Come over to our side. We've got some absolute values you've never heard about.

Now a person who goes to the theatre wants nothing better than to be on the side of somebody who is already on the stage. If any chance is provided by the show, the spectator will be able to forget his own life and yield to the appeal of an imaginary one. "Living theatre," of course, wants a somewhat different effect. It wants to touch the spectator directly in his own life without his having forgotten it. But can this be achieved by begging him to change his views? To what views? No new ones are proposed. What is the spectator to do? Is he to contribute to the Living Theatre? Become a member of its cast? During *The Apple,* an actor tells the audience that anyone wishing a part should leave his name at the box office.

But what occurs during the performance of *The Apple* that could possibly excite the desire of a spectator to take part in it? At least in *The Connection* we saw people taking drugs to music. That was something definite. Besides, the action in the play presented a real milieu, to which, things being what they are, one might conceivably want to belong. In *The Apple* there is no real milieu, nor is there any action; no goal is proposed by anybody other than the desire to disconcert the audience. A spastic is insulted by a drunk, a dummy is operated on, a "drip" painting is dripped on glass, the drunk dies, the spastic reveals that he is not really a spastic but was merely acting. Finally, the message of the play is delivered by the actor who at the outset had promised the audience dire things if it stayed to the end:

You know, something dies and something is born. A little of the old faces and a few of the new. It could be you up here. There's only one necessary ingredient. You got to want. I don't care if you want a meal or if you come to steal. It'll work itself out. One way or the other. Look at this apple. . . . You can tell a lot of people wanted this apple because it's all chewed up. It's a good thing. . . . Now don't come back without wanting something. Hear me? Okay, Okay. . . .

Isn't this speech one the audience might have addressed to the actors on the stage? For it is a law of the stage that people on it must want something. After all, it was his understanding of this law that made Corneille a great playwright. Moreover, Samuel Beckett's refusal to accept this law has made him an inadequate playwright, except in *Waiting for Godot,* where his characters at least "want" something: to wait. Now in *The Apple* we see people on the stage who want nothing, but who yet lecture the audience on the desirability of "wanting." The audience, by being in the theatre, has indicated that it wants something. I think it wants to see a play.

I take it, though, that the play's message is not just the admonition to "want." The message really is: Why don't you want to be like us? What is wrong with you? But after the clumsy antics of *The Apple*'s performers, who could prefer their lot to his own? Evidently, some can.

We have recently had in New York a phenomenon called "Happenings." These are improvised performances put on mainly in painters' studios and mainly by painters. Why not? In a new play by Jean Genet the actors are required to paint the sets. So why shouldn't painters act? But do the actors of "Happenings" act? Apparently they do now, for these things, having caught on, are now rehearsed. For instance, in a "Happening" done by the Living Theatre itself on a Monday night, a girl—Japanese—made love to a piano —placed on its backside. Another gimmick, of course. . . . *The Apple* could be best described as a collage of "Happenings."

Is the Living Theatre wrong to have concentrated at this time on one theatrical effect? One aim is better than two or three, if it is, in fact, the best aim possible. But if what is aimed at is clearly secondary, or tangential in the whole order of theatrical effects, then to make of that aim something absolute is a sign of poverty not riches, of weakness not strength.

I think, too, that "living theatre" can have only as much life as its audiences bring to it. The effect it specializes in requires good, that is to say, lively audiences. But the plays the Living Theatre has chosen for production have suggested in the main—*The Apple* most emphatically—that any audience, *qua* audience, is dead. If the real show appears in the self-consciousness of the public, a self-consciousness the play serves merely to stimulate, then that public must be already real and not hungering for some "reality" it can find only on the stage. Brecht did not think his audience wanted nothing; perhaps he thought it wanted capitalism; he wanted to change this want, or to substitute a new object for it: Communism. Brecht did not think his spectators dead; he thought them mistaken. With a dead audience, how can there be life on any stage? And of all stages, that of the Living Theatre?

Jack Gelber told reporters that the theme of *The Apple* is death. And it is: death taken abstractly, in its opposition to life as such, no matter how purposeless. But life without purpose is indistinguishable from death, and there can be no real conflict between death and death. Life is "really" life only when it goes against its own tendency to be indeterminate and anomalous, only when it sets itself a goal, only when it wants to do something more than to just go on living. And even the message of *The Apple*—Be an imbecile—could have been meaningful if intended—it was not —as a protest against life's boring and protoplasmic trend toward indeterminateness. It has been said than an intelligent person in the modern world can no longer set himself a goal. In that case, I suggest, intelligent people should set themselves the goal of being a little less intelligent. But the self-chastisement of reason is something very different from the crass and blatant assertion of sheer mindlessness. The message of *The Apple* is far indeed from the rueful wisdom with which Gogol's play *The Gamblers* terminates, when the professional, who has been cheated by even sharper sharpers, sums up the truth of his experience as follows: "My mother told me when I was young: If you are stupid, be resigned to being stupid; but if you happen to be intelligent, try, try to be stupid."

Samuel Beckett and James Joyce
in Endgame

AFTER THAT marvelous wondering at the world which the performance of Samuel Beckett's *Waiting for Godot* occasioned, came a wondering at certain characteristics of the play itself, which, not being clear in their purpose or meaning, puzzled without astonishing. When the curtain was rung down on *Godot,* a certain number of questions remained. Who was Godot? Why were Vladimir and Estragon waiting for him? Why were Pozzo and Lucky in the play at all, since they seemed to have no definite relation to the two tramps? Why was Lucky's famous "thinking speech" a parody of James Joyce? Finally, was the mood of the play one of despair or of hope?

Some of these questions can now be answered. Samuel Beckett's subsequent play, *Endgame,* treating the same experience dealt with in *Godot,* illuminates, at least speculatively, much that remained obscure in the latter, and most surprisingly. *Endgame,* though less effective on the stage, is superior in many respects to *Waiting for Godot;* it is purer in form, denser in meaning, a deeper expression of Samuel Beckett's ultimate purposes. *Endgame* is one long act where *Godot* was somewhat repetitious in two. Those who felt that Beckett's talent does not lie in dramatic construction, contrivance of plot, or development of character—at least, as customarily understood—and would be best expressed in the simpler rhythm of a single act are justified by the proportions of the more recent play.

So much for the question of form. My question, though, was: who is Pozzo? And the answer to this question, which *Endgame* makes possible, provides a key to other questions which *Godot* provoked. Pozzo, it will be remembered, was the man with a whip driving the slave, Lucky, before him, who burst onto the scene to terrify, entertain, and in a way console the two tramps, Estragon and Vladimir. It will be remembered, too, that when he reappears, he has gone blind and he speaks poetically (in a manner which seems out of keeping with the ferocious character he has shown) of the nonexistence of time, and the all-encompassing power of eternity. Hearing that speech in the theatre, I had a distinct impulse to believe that Pozzo himself was Godot, the Mysterious Personage the two tramps were waiting to see, and who both felt could possibly justify their sad and trivial existences. In the end, however, this did not seem to be the case. From *Endgame* I think I have learned that Pozzo is none other than Beckett's former literary master and friend, James Joyce.

This play is directly and undeviatingly about Joyce and Beckett's relationship to him. It is abundantly clear now why Lucky, in his monologue, parodied the Joycean manner. There are any number of such parodies in *Endgame*, and by the central character, Hamm. (In this very name there is a suggestion that Shem and Shaun were just masks, that the real personality was Hamm-Joyce.) Whereas in *Godot* it was Lucky—that is, Beckett—who parodied Joyce, in *Endgame*, it is Hamm—that is, Joyce himself—who does the parodying.

Hamm is, among other things, the ham actor of the story of his life. He is blind, like Joyce, and tyrannical, yet human; he is cruel and yet with great dignity. His associate in *Endgame* is a younger man, Clov, who is apparently his adopted son. Clov (Beckett) is the less human of the two. He is the younger, the less ailing, and he has at least one hope; Hamm has none. Clov's hope is that he may some day leave Hamm. On this topic Hamm is humorous: "Without Hamm no home." In fact, in *Endgame* there is no home without Hamm, for the attic, which he shares with Clov, is all that remains of the world, everything else having been destroyed. "Why don't you kill me?" he asks Clov. "Because I don't have the key," Clov answers. This is the key to their cupboard. I think it is also the key to literary pre-eminence. A strange ménage, certainly, as Rimbaud remarked of his relationship with Verlaine, and like that relationship, literary in essence.

For Hamm is a writer; he is apparently occupied with a Work in Progress, and surely with this detail Beckett wants us to identify him as Joyce. This work is also the story of his own life. Perhaps it is even the story of how Clov-Beckett became Hamm-Joyce's son.

As in *Godot,* there are two other characters. But in *Endgame* the two extra characters are definitely related to the principals. The subordinate characters are Hamm's parents —his father, Nagg, and his mother, Nell, both of whom have lost their feet in an accident. Hamm keeps them in ashcans, sometimes getting Clov to lift the lids of the cans to inspect or feed or annoy them, as in this wonderful instance:

HAMM: It's time for my story. Do you want to listen to my story?
CLOV: No.

HAMM: Ask my father if he wants to listen to my story.
(Clov goes to the bins, raises the lid of Nagg's, stoops, looks
into it. Pause. He straightens up.)
    CLOV: He's asleep.
    HAMM: Wake him. (Clov stoops, wakes Nagg with the alarm.
Unintelligible words. Clov straightens up.)
    CLOV: He doesn't want to listen to your story.
    HAMM: I'll give him a bonbon. (Clov stoops. As before.)
    CLOV: He wants a sugarplum.
    HAMM: He'll get a sugarplum. (Clov stoops. As before.)
    CLOV: It's a deal. . . .

Hamm, in this scene, wants to tell his father, Nagg, the
story of his life, and the father can only be persuaded to
listen to it by a pitiful bribe. All of Joyce's megalomania
and cruelty are in the episode. Beckett has not spared his
master any more than Clov would have spared Hamm, or
than Lucky would spare Pozzo if he were able to over-
power him finally. And from this comes the suggestion that
like Hamm, Pozzo was Beckett's image of Joyce, only more
caricatured in the first than in the second play. In fact,
Hamm is a mixture of Pozzo and Vladimir, while Clov is
a mixture of Estragon and Lucky.

Certainly, very few who saw *Godot* could have suspected
that the experience of the two central characters symbolized
so literary a relationship as the one that obtained between
Joyce and Beckett. Who could have imagined, when in-
duced to pity for the two tramps, and to terror by the spec-
tacle of the master with a whip, that Beckett was bespeak-
ing his own literary friendship with the author of *Ulysses*?
The core of Beckett's experience as revealed by *Endgame*
can be summed up as follows: The worst thing that happened to Beckett was also the best thing that happened to
him—his encounter with Joyce.

We can only speculate about their relationship, to be
sure, but on the other hand we do know something about
the two men. Beckett came to Paris as a young man interested in writing modernist poetry and fiction. Joyce was
then the top figure of the whole modernist movement. He
was the acknowledged master, the king of language, the
great innovator, the destroyer of old forms and the con-
temnor of old values. He had more pride than any other
writer of the time, and he was more self-absorbed, too,

being the very figure of a man dedicated to himself. For Joyce had little interest in other writers. Stephen Daedalus remarks in *Ulysses:* "His own image to a man with that queer thing genius is the standard of all experience, material and moral. Such an appeal will touch him. The images of other males of his blood will repel him. He will see in them grotesque attempts of nature to foretell or repeat himself." Now it is simply not true that all men of genius react in this manner toward other men. But Joyce did, no doubt of it.

And this was the man Beckett chose to be his literary father. Beckett did show Joyce his work. In fact, what I get from a study of the plays is that in Beckett's mind Joyce became Beckett's one family relation, his adopted father. And apparently it was Beckett who adopted Joyce —not Joyce Beckett, though Hamm in *Endgame* claims to have adopted Clov.

Joyce wrote, and abundantly, of his own father and mother. Beckett—in his plays at least—only about himself and Joyce, and, in *Endgame*, of Joyce's father and mother. According to Richard Ellmann's book, *James Joyce*, the great writer once said to Beckett directly: "I don't love anyone except my family," in a tone which Ellmann notes suggested that he didn't *like* anyone except his family either. But if Joyce wrote of his own father and mother, and in every one of his books, Beckett never writes in his plays of his parents—only of Joyce's. Had they by then become Beckett's grandparents?

Perhaps it was because Beckett had adopted Joyce as his literary father that he did not want him for a real-life father-in-law. When, according to Ellmann's account, Joyce's daughter Lucia felt impelled to reveal to Beckett the passion she felt for him, "Beckett told her bluntly that he came to the Joyce flat primarily to see her father." (The effect on Lucia was catastrophic.) Maybe he meant to say, *"My* father."

To have adopted such a man as Joyce shows two things about Beckett which are evidenced in other ways throughout his work: first, a desire to be destroyed, and secondly, contradicting that desire, limitless self-confidence. When we consider how many men have been ruined because their fathers had too much power or personality, we can better appreciate what Beckett's daring must have been in adopting as his literary master and single human relation the mighty, coolly indifferent, and self-absorbed literary giant.

Beckett did, in fact, make many efforts to get away from Joyce. All of his novels are, I think, flights from Joyce—perhaps toward Kafka. Beckett's essay on Proust is also a flight from Joyce, and an ineffectual one. Proust is not described personally in the essay, nor does Kafka appear as a character in *Malone, Malone Dies,* or *Murphy.* But Joyce is present in Beckett's plays; he is confronted and he is vanquished, though Beckett, whether as Lucky or as Clov, is never shown to be victorious. Yet Joyce as Pozzo is blinded; as Hamm, he is deserted by Clov and left to die. On the other hand, Joyce, whether as Hamm or Pozzo, is always more sympathetic and more human than whoever speaks for Beckett, be this Lucky or Clov.

Can we now say who Godot is? For those who saw the play performed, he may be a mythical being and stand for whatever unattainable thing they might be waiting for. My suggestion, though, derives from my first impression that Pozzo, whom I identified as Joyce, was, in fact, Godot: Godot would be Joyce if Beckett had never met him; Godot would be Beckett if Beckett had never had to admire Joyce.

Another question: Do these plays express despair or hope? This, too, has to be answered speculatively. The extraordinary thing about *Endgame* and *Godot* is that they are capable of moving people who have not the faintest conception of what the relations between two writers, one young and aspiring, the other world-renowned, could be. It does strike me that the plays are more despairing than hopeful; yet they induce an exhilaration we could scarcely get from pessimistic works. Are they tragic, then? Not quite. And yet . . . there is tragedy somewhere near the characters, not in them. Perhaps the tragedy has already occurred, and Beckett's figures, Hamm and Clov, Pozzo and Lucky, Estragon and Vladimir, are merely members of the chorus. Nell and Nagg are a chorus at a still further remove. It is the chorus which expresses the drastic pessimism of Sophocles' tragedies, never the protagonists who endure the agony. Beckett and Joyce were after all writers, scribes: Whatever happened between them could not be tragic except in the derived way discovered by Samuel Beckett, and which has made both of his plays authentic and extraordinary works. There have not been many such since *Finnegans Wake*, which was intended, I suspect, to make any masterpiece after it impossible.

The Theatre and the "Absurd"

IS THE WORLD we live in "absurd"? And has it become so recently? And does our world, newly absurd, require a particular kind of theatrical art expressing "absurdity"?

If you are ready to answer "yes," then you are likely to be convinced by what Martin Esslin says in his book, *The Theatre of the Absurd.*

Esslin says that our present sense of absurdity springs from the loss of humanly important realities. Of what realities? Well, Esslin thinks we have lost God. I should like to know when this occurred. But Esslin probably means merely that we have lost a belief in God once natural to us. Now I confess to having very little nostalgia for those periods of history when it was "natural" to believe in God. Was such belief ever really natural? Sören Kierkegaard, for one, thought that Christian education, "natural" in the nineteenth century—this kind of education we have lost—was the main obstacle to Christian belief; for Kierkegaard, true belief was always possible, always miraculous.

Is the family gone? At least it is better understood. Is the State gone? But the State seems to require the efforts and adherence of the young, and more than ever. Is patriotism gone? If so, is the loss grievous? Yet the figure of Colonel John Glenn, so much with us at this moment, suggests that patriotism still has no little virility. The cosmonaut, who orbited the earth three times and saw four settings of the sun in a few hours, came back to earth to inform us that he is still thrilled by the sight of the American flag. Did he then go up into weightless space just for the sake of a fractious parcel of humanity confined to United States territory in the Western Hemisphere? If so, his exploit must frighten us, much as it thrills us. What a man can do so well, he still does not do for men. The world is not so different from what it was.

Is reason gone? Then who would infer anything from our loss of it? To say that reason is gone is to speak without any hope of being understood. An absurd world would be silent; it would not be plied with plays.

Esslin makes much of another loss: that of our formerly felt intimacy with the world. And in support, he quotes from Camus' *The Myth of Sisyphus*:

A world that can be explained by reasoning, however faulty, is a familiar world. But in a universe that is suddenly deprived of illusions and of light, man feels a stranger. His is an irremediable exile, because he is deprived of memories of a lost homeland as much as he lacks hope of a promised land to come. This divorce between man and his life, the actor and his setting, truly constitutes the feeling of absurdity.

I think it is absurd to take anyone—even Camus—for an authority on the "absurd." And, in fact, the quotation above, which Esslin has used to buttress his view, is fairly close to nonsense. Imagine: Camus prefers a world that can be explained by faulty reasoning—but why then use the term "explained"?—to one inexplicable by good reasoning. He wants the world to be familiar; Aristotle thought it should excite wonder. And how could the world ever be deprived of illusion, which is so large a part of it? Camus himself had plenty of illusions, one of them being that we are bound to have a feeling of absurdity if denied the memory of "a lost homeland" and of "a promised land come." Is it absurd not to have had a good background or to be without real prospects? Sad, perhaps; but it is one thing to call the world sad, quite another to call it "absurd." The first statement is without philosophical pretension.

The world can no more become absurd than it can sin, starve, or fall down. There are many absurdities in the world; most of them were always there.

But was there always a Theatre of the Absurd? I claim there was not and that there is no such thing now. Esslin claims that (1) there was a Theatre of the Absurd in the past and (2) the group of contemporary dramatists whom he has singled out write the kinds of plays they do in response to a particular crisis the world is going through at this time. But the two claims refute each other. Esslin maintains that there is a particular spiritual crisis, and that a certain kind of dramatic art has been produced in order to express it; but he cannot maintain, then, that forms of theatre like those being produced now long antedated the crisis. Yet in a chapter entitled "The Tradition of the Absurd," Esslin ranges through past history for prototypes of the new kinds of plays now being written. The mimes of the Middle Ages, the court jesters, the clowns of Shakespeare, the harlequinades which entered into the British music hall and American vaudeville, the Commedia dell'Arte, the nonsense verse of Lear and Lewis Carroll are all called on to account for the character of specifically modern works, which character, in turn, is supposed to be due to a special contemporary predicament. Esslin writes: "This is not the place for a detailed study of Shakespearean clowns, fools, and ruffians as forerunners of the Theatre of the Absurd." No, it is not.

But let us consider Esslin's main contention that there is a Theatre of the Absurd at this time, quite apart from his other contention that it pre-existed its own *raison d'être*. Is it true that Beckett, Ionesco, Adamov, Genet, Albee, Arrabal, Grass, Pinter, and Simpson can be best understood if considered as instigators of a new theatrical art, the Theatre of the Absurd? Some of the playwrights listed above have, to be sure, written plays to Esslin's specifications, but only one of these, Ionesco, is really important. The three major figures, as I am sure Esslin himself would agree, are Ionesco, Beckett, and Genet. But of these three, only Ionesco fits Esslin's formula.

One individual, to be sure, if an artist of rank, has as much interest as a whole school. And Ionesco is a remarkable playwright with some five or six masterpieces to his credit. He has great invention and an exuberant humor; unfortunately, his ideas are topical, adventitious: the last thing one could say about them is that they are "new." One typically "new" idea of Ionesco's is that there are no new ideas, even in the construction of plays. Here he is quite wrong. He has written some plays that are really novel as structures. It is the ideas expressed in them that are all too familiar and which spring from the prevailing climate of political and metaphysical pessimism.

What is objectionable in Ionesco's theatre is curiously akin to what is objectionable in Esslin's whole concept. Ionesco thinks absurdity is something new;* Esslin wants to give us news of the absurd.

Esslin talks a lot about Samuel Beckett and Jean Genet. But in the fairly detailed analyses he makes of their lives and work he is unable to illuminate much of their art or even to give us the feeling that he has judged it wisely.

Beckett he discusses under this rubric: "The Search for the Self." And Esslin searches accordingly in Richard Ellmann's biography of James Joyce (who knew Beckett) for such data as might throw light on *Waiting for Godot* and *Endgame*. Now Ellmann's book is valuable on Beckett as well as Joyce. For instance, it appears that Beckett is given to long silences and when he visited Joyce they often stared at each other for hours without uttering a word. This certainly tells us something about the kind of dialogue we have come to expect from Beckett. But what has the personal data about Beckett to do with a general cultural crisis, or with any modern feeling for absurdity? Beckett is a very strange man, no question of that. Even his handwriting, of which I have seen one instance, is peculiar in the extreme.

Esslin finds fault with my own view expressed in a piece I did on Beckett for *The New Leader*: "Samuel Beckett and James Joyce in *Endgame*," and in which I attempted to explain Beckett's play in terms of his attitude to James Joyce. Esslin says that my theory "surely becomes untenable"; not because there may not be a certain amount of truth · in it (every writer is bound to use elements of his own experience of life in his work) but because, far from illuminating the full content of a play like *Endgame*, such an interpretation reduces it to a trivial level." Did I reduce the relationship between Hamm and Clov to a trivial level? I made the point that the *value* of recognizing the autobiographical material in the play was that by so doing, it was possible to absolve the author of the charge of pessimism. But never mind my own interpretation of the play.

* I don't think Ionesco regards "absurdity" as an *idea*, but as *anti-idea*. His theatre has been called "antitheatre."

Here is Esslin's: "The experience expressed in Beckett's plays (including *Endgame*) is of a far more profound and fundamental nature than mere autobiography. They reveal his experience of temporality and evanescence; his sense of the tragic difficulty of becoming aware of one's own self in the merciless process of renovation and destruction that occurs with change in time; of the difficulty of communication between human beings; of the unending quest for reality in a world in which everything is uncertain and the borderline between dream and reality is ever shifting: of the tragic nature of all love relationships and the self-deception of friendship . . . and so on." Are Beckett's plays about all that? From this list of abstractions one would think that Beckett's plays had been written in the German language and not, exquisitely, in the French. Besides, what have Esslin's list of abstractions to do with the life of Samuel Beckett? And what has that life to do with a general cultural crisis? These are the connections Esslin is obliged to establish, and he does not.

On the subject of Genet, too, Esslin's concept of the absurd is little help. He turns to the data about Genet's life which we have from the playwright himself. It seems that Genet was abandoned as a child, and when accused of stealing, resolved to become a thief. Between 1930 and 1940, as Esslin notes, Genet led the life of an itinerant delinquent, among beggars and pimps; he made acquaintance with the French jails. Fortunately for the theatre, he never quite became "the hardened jail-bird on whom the prison gates shut forever." *

These facts show Genet to be a very strange person, too. Should not his personal strangeness be related to his plays? But Esslin, out to prove his theory, disregards the personal facts and concentrates on the "absurdity of our historical epoch." He derives Genet's plays from the modern feeling of helplessness in facing a mechanized world. Esslin writes: "A feeling of helplessness when confronted with the vast intricacy of the modern world, and the individual's impotence in making his own influence felt on that intricate and mysterious machinery, pervades the consciousness of Western man today. A world that functions mysteriously outside our conscious control must appear absurd." Once

* Rimbaud, *A Season in Hell.*

again Esslin has trotted out fashionable and very misleading clichés. The world Genet describes in his plays is the product of a virile imagination, almost Elizabethan in its force and fancy. Genet could be compared to Marlowe, never to Kafka.

Art, it must be admitted, is unable to occupy a central position in the modern world; thus, the artist cannot be in the very center of things. But Homer was certainly in the very center of things Greek when he wrote the *Iliad*, although he wrote it in Ionian; and Sophocles was in the center of the Greek world when he wrote plays for the Athenian public. In the modern world, of course, no such privileged position is open to art. To look at all, the artist is probably condemned not to look all around him. Can anyone be in the center of things in our age? This is not sure. But this is sure: anyone who is will not be an artist. That is why a Homer is utterly inconceivable today. (Hegel notes that there was not a single tool made by the Greeks which went unremarked in Homer's *Iliad*. Is it conceivable that any modern poet could sum up in song all the instruments manufactured in our society? Besides, to carry Hegel's point further, every tool Homer described was already an art object.) Very probably art requires, if it is to be practiced at all today, that its creator contribute to it his own personal oddity. I suggest that this is a logical consequence of the marginal situation of art as such. Political criticism of art, even when sensitive and cultivated, has proved utterly sterile and unable to instigate any sort of new creation. It was based on a fallacy: that politics was central (this is certainly to be questioned) and that being central, it had the right to insist that art be central, also; now two things cannot occupy the same place at the same time—perhaps they can if infinitely smaller than miniscule. But the political critics of modern art and literature were not thinking along the lines of quantum physics. They were thinking of the art produced in past epochs when art *was* central. In fact, the history of what we call modern art and modern literature has been the successive imposition on the public of bizarre standpoints, unexpected attitudes, peculiar effects. This has gone on for a fairly long time but it has only recently become a general trend in the theatre. Of course, Strindberg was as peculiar as Beckett or Genet; but he was more exceptional in the early part of this century. It is now to be expected that personally peculiar people will create the art which persons of sensibility are able to enjoy. Does this mean that a theatre created by "peculiar" persons should be called the Theatre of the Absurd?

I think the important point to make here is that this development in the theatre is belated, and follows some fifty or seventy years after personal oddity had vindicated itself in other fields—painting, poetry, and the novel—as essential to the production of authentic art. In fact, I would suggest that one reason good art has for so long a time been "advanced" art is that artists relished the freakishness attendant on being "ahead" of others. One way of being peculiar is to be in advance like the crane who, Lautréamont says, flying first, forces all the others to look at its behind.

But for the theatre—and Esslin does not see this at all—the need to be bizarre, eccentric, individual involves the creator in a dialectic, as it perhaps does not involve any other type of creator—painter, poet, or novelist. Admitted that it is an advantage if you want to create to be personally strange: still, in the theatre your personal strangeness has to have an immediate effect on an audience composed of very different persons, who have to react to the play presented before they have had a chance to be converted to it by the intimidating force of cultural opinion. I do not think the dialectic I have indicated should come to an end. I think it is this dialectic which has made the plays of both Beckett and Genet more available to us than their novels were. If Beckett had not turned to the theatre, he would have remained the eccentric writer of morbid tales in monotonous, if good, prose. If Genet had not turned to the play form, he would have remained a writer of lyrical pornography. The dialectic imposed by the theatre has made it possible for these "strangers" to speak in a language pleasing both to them and to us. It is this dialectic which makes the new plays more interesting to me, at least, than the new poems or novels. Of all modern works it is the new theatre pieces which are, and have to be, I suggest, the least "absurd."

DRAMABOOKS

SD 3 *The Chinese Wall* by Max Frisch
SD 4 *Billy Budd* by Louis O. Coxe and Robert Chapman
SD 5 *The Devils* by John Whiting
SD 6 *The Firebugs* by Max Frisch

CRITICISM

D 1 *Shakespeare and the Elizabethans* by Henri Fluchère
D 2 *On Dramatic Method* by Harley Granville-Barker
D 3 *George Bernard Shaw* by G. K. Chesterton
D 4 *The Paradox of Acting* by Denis Diderot and *Masks or Faces?* by William Archer
D 5 *The Scenic Art* by Henry James
D 6 *Preface to Hamlet* by Harley Granville-Barker
D 7 *Hazlitt on Theatre* edited by William Archer and Robert Lowe
D 8 *The Fervent Years* by Harold Clurman
D 9 *The Quintessence of Ibsenism* by Bernard Shaw
D 10 *Papers on Playmaking* edited by Brander Matthews
D 11 *Papers on Acting* edited by Brander Matthews
D 12 *The Theatre* by Stark Young
D 13 *Immortal Shadows* by Stark Young
D 14 *Shakespeare: A Survey* by E. K. Chambers
D 15 *The English Dramatic Critics* edited by James Agate
D 16 *Japanese Theatre* by Faubion Bowers
D 17 *Shaw's Dramatic Criticism (1895-98)* edited by John F. Matthews
D 18 *Shaw on Theatre* edited by E. J. West
D 19 *The Book of Job as a Greek Tragedy* by Horace Meyer Kallen
D 20 *Molière: The Man Seen Through the Plays* by Ramon Fernandez
D 21 *Greek Tragedy* by Gilbert Norwood
D 22 *Samuel Johnson on Shakespeare* edited by W. K. Wimsatt, Jr.
D 23 *The Poet in the Theatre* by Ronald Peacock
D 24 *Chekhov the Dramatist* by David Magarshack
D 25 *Theory and Technique of Playwriting* by John Howard Lawson
D 26 *The Art of the Theatre* by Henri Ghéon
D 27 *Aristotle's Poetics* with an Introduction by Francis Fergusson
D 28 *The Origin of the Theater* by Benjamin Hunningher
D 29 *Playwrights on Playwriting* by Toby Cole
D 30 *The Sense of Shakespeare's Sonnets* by Edward Hubler
D 31 *The Development of Shakespeare's Imagery* by Wolfgang Clemen
D 32 *Stanislavsky on the Art of the Stage* translated by David Magarshack
D 33 *Metatheatre: A New View of Dramatic Form* by Lionel Abel